FLOODS

DANGEROUS WEATHER

FLOODS

Michael Allaby

☑®
Facts On File, Inc.

FLOODS

Copyright © 1998 by Michael Allaby

Facts On File, Inc.
11 Penn Plaza
New York NY 10001

Library of Congress Cataloging-in-Publication Data
Allaby, Michael.
   Floods / Michael Allaby.
     p. cm. — (Dangerous weather)
   Includes index.
   Summary: Presents information on these most damaging of all natural disasters from the perspective of basic meteorology and environmental science, including floodplains, aquifers, tsunamis, the cost of floods, and prevention.
    ISBN 0-8160-3520-2 (alk. paper)
    1. Floods—Juvenile literature. [1. Floods.] I. Title. II. Series: Allaby, Michael. Dangerous weather.
   GB1399.A45 1998
   551.48'9—dc21   97-18374

Facts On File books are available at special discounts when purchased in bulk quantities for businesses, associations, institutions or sales promotions. Please call our Special Sales Department in New York at (212) 967-8800 or (800) 322-8755.

You can find Facts On File on the World Wide Web at http://www.factsonfile.com

Text design by Richard Garratt
Layout by Robert Yaffe
Cover design by Matt Galemmo

Printed in the United States of America

RRD FOF 10 9 8 7 6 5

This book is printed on acid-free paper.

Contents

FLOODS

What is a flood?

It had been raining for days on end throughout most of October, and the citizens of Florence, Italy, were longing for the weather to improve. They began to hope it might when November began with two fine days, but on November 3 the rains returned with a vengeance. In just 48 hours, 19 inches (48.26 centimeters) of rain fell on the city. It also fell on the Apennines, the mountain range that runs like a spine down the center of Italy. Water flowing off the mountains is carried away by rivers that eventually join the Arno, the river that flows 150 miles (240 kilometers) from the mountains to the Mediterranean and passes through Florence. The year was 1966.

Often, the Arno carries so little water it is almost dry, but the river is treacherous. Over the centuries it has overflowed its banks countless times, whenever heavy rain has sent water cascading down the mountain slopes across bare, impermeable clay. On the night of November 3, the reservoir behind a hydroelectric dam was filling rapidly, and to protect the dam, a great surge of water was

Figure 1: *In Hanoi, Vietnam, a nearly submerged taxi struggles on a street flooded by tropical storm Frankie, July 24, 1996.* (Reuters/Dylan Martinez/Archive Photos)

released suddenly. This arrived at a second hydroelectric dam farther downstream, and at about 9 P.M. excess water was released from it into the Arno.

Down in Florence, many people had gone to bed early. They did not see the rate at which the river level was rising. It flooded the sewers, driving sewage through manholes and onto the streets, then burst through walls. All the power supplies failed, and at 7:26 A.M. every mains-powered electric clock stopped. Oil storage tanks were broken open by the battering waters, and oil mixed with the mud that had been swept down from the hills. By dawn on November 4, floodwaters were flowing through the city; they continued to flow for several hours. The torrential rain also continued to fall. In places the dirty water was 20 feet (6 meters) deep, and 100,000 people were trapped on the upper floors of buildings. Prisoners at the Santa Teresa prison were taken to the roof, where they overpowered their guards but remained imprisoned by the swirling waters on all sides. Every road and rail line into the city was blocked. When a party sent by the government in Rome managed to enter the city at about 6:00 P.M., one of them described the Piazza San Marco as a "storm-tossed lake."

When, at last, the waters subsided, Florence lay beneath a thick layer of mud mixed with oil. Florence, renowned for its beautiful churches, museums, and galleries, which together house some of the world's most important art treasures, is also the site of Italy's largest library, the Biblioteca Nazionale Centrale. All were flooded. Books and manuscripts were soaked, paintings covered in oily mud. A huge international effort was mounted to recover as much as possible from the tragedy. The work of restoration still continues, and a great deal of the damage has been repaired.

This was one of the most serious floods of modern times, but famous only because it struck at such an important cultural center. Fortunately, only 35 people died, and had no art treasures been at risk, the disaster would have been quickly forgotten. All floods leave behind a thick carpet of mud and slime to add to the damage caused by the water itself, but in most cases the victims are ordinary people, and many floods claim far more lives than the one that devastated Florence in 1966.

In July 1996, for example, hundreds of people are believed to have died in North Korea, after 20 inches (50.8 centimeters) of rain—in places, 29 inches (73.7 centimeters)—fell in five days. In the same month the state government in Assam, India, had to set up relief camps for 1.5 million people who lost their homes when floods inundated 60 villages. China suffered even worse destruction at about the same time. More than 1,500 people died in floods that were 20 feet (6 meters) deep. Floods destroy not only buildings and roads. They also destroy food. The Chinese floods destroyed at least

2.5 million acres (1 million hectares) of crops, and the Korean floods affected the main rice-growing areas.

Nor do the rains arrive alone. The fierce storms that cause heavy rain also bring strong winds. Tropical cyclones, known as hurricanes in the Atlantic and Caribbean, typhoons in Asia, and cyclones in the Bay of Bengal, are the most ferocious of all storms, and also bring the heaviest rain, 20 inches (50.8 centimeters) in 48 hours being fairly common. A typhoon once brought more than 60 inches (152.4 centimeters) of rain to the Philippines.

Rain is fresh water, but the sea can also inundate coastal areas. Tropical cyclones form over the ocean; if they cross a coast they usually cause a storm surge, when the low pressure makes the sea level rise and hurricane-force onshore winds produce huge waves.

The most terrifying of all sea waves, however, is the tsunami, or "harbor wave," often known, incorrectly (because it has nothing to do with the tide), as a "tidal wave." A tsunami arrives suddenly, traveling with immense speed, as a series of solid walls of water that demolish everything in their path (see page 54).

Historically, floods have caused more damage and killed more people than any other kind of natural disaster. They may be less sensational than hurricanes and less horrifying than tornadoes, but they are far more frequent than either, and they are confined to no particular regions of the world. They can, and do, happen anywhere.

Evaporation, precipitation, and transpiration

Whether salt or fresh, all the water on Earth comes from the sea and returns to it in an endless cycle called the hydrologic, or water, cycle. When the floodwaters sweep through streets and homes, they may come from a river that has burst its banks, but ultimately the water that fills the river, and the rain that supplies it, comes from the ocean.

The oceans are the reservoir of the planet. They cover almost 71 percent of the surface of the Earth to an average depth of a little more than 2 miles (3.2 kilometers), and they contain nearly 330 million cubic miles (1.35 billion cubic kilometers) of water. This is all salt water, of course. In addition, the polar icecaps and glaciers contain about 10 million cubic miles (41 million cubic kilometers) of water. That is fresh water, but we cannot use it. We must rely on the water in lakes and rivers and below the surface of dry land:

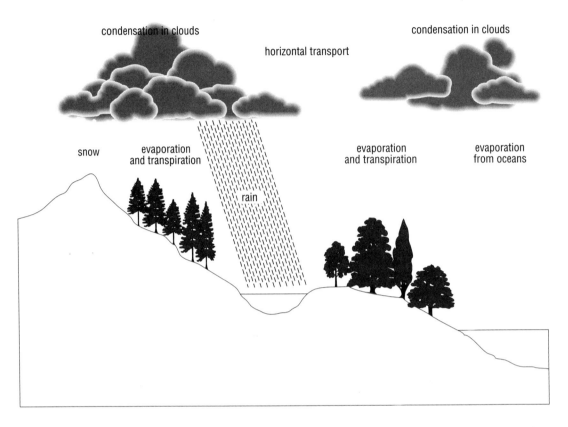

condensation in clouds

condensation in clouds

horizontal transport

snow

evaporation and transpiration

rain

evaporation and transpiration

evaporation from oceans

Figure 2: *The hydrologic cycle.*

a total of about 3.5 million cubic miles (14.35 million cubic kilometers), or about 1 percent of all the water on the planet. At any one time the atmosphere contains about 1.2 million cubic miles (4.92 cubic kilometers) of water vapor and cloud droplets. All the clouds in the world, and all the invisible water vapor in the air, together amount to no more than about 0.3 percent of all the water on Earth.

As figure 2 shows, water is constantly moving from the surface to the air and back again. That movement constitutes the cycle, but the length of time an individual water molecule remains in one part of the cycle varies widely. When the molecule enters the air, it remains there an average of 9 or 10 days before it falls as rain or snow. When it falls, it may evaporate again almost immediately, but if it falls on dry land it may soak into the ground and enter an aquifer (see page 21). It may spend only a few days there if the aquifer is not far below the surface and made of a substance such as gravel, through which water flows easily, but there are some deep aquifers in which water can spend millions of years. A water molecule may remain in a river for only a few days, but if the river carries it into a big lake, it may stay there for decades. Water that falls as snow may form part of an ice sheet or glacier. On one of the polar ice sheets, a molecule may be trapped for hundreds of thousands of years, but a small glacier will retain the molecule for only a few decades. Once the molecule enters the ocean, it is likely to remain there for up to 3,000 years.

The average time a water molecule spends in one part of the cycle is called its "residence time." Except for water that is trapped in aquifers deep below ground, the residence time is proportional to the amount of water present in each stage of the cycle. The air contains little water, so molecules remain there only briefly. Ice sheets and the oceans contain much more water, and water remains in them for a long time.

The amount of water at each stage in the cycle is not completely constant. During ice ages, the ice sheets and glaciers expand to cover a much larger area than they do today, and the residence time of water molecules in them is greater than that for liquid water, carried by rivers and aquifers. Water accumulates in the ice sheets, and the amount held in the oceans decreases. Sea levels fall as water moves from one major reservoir to another. When an ice age ends and the ice sheets melt, their water returns to the oceans and sea levels rise again.

Most of the time, however, the cycle is in balance. Water evaporates. Once in the air, the water vapor condenses to form clouds, and water returns to the surface as rain or snow. Rivers carry water back to the sea—the same amount of water as fell over land from clouds formed of water evaporated from the sea. A small amount of water is lost into space from the top of the atmosphere, where it escapes the gravitational pull of the Earth. This is balanced by "juvenile" water released from volcanoes.

"Precipitation" is the name meteorologists use to describe water falling from clouds, regardless of whether it is liquid or solid or the size of its flakes or drops. Rain, drizzle, sleet, snow, hail, and fog are all types of precipitation.

Most precipitation falls into the oceans. Oceans cover a much larger area than land, and it is from the oceans that most water evaporates. On average, about 210 cubic miles, or 861 cubic kilometers, of water (85 percent of the total evaporation) evaporate from the oceans every day, and about 38 cubic miles, or 155.8 cubic kilometers (15 percent) enter the air from land by evaporation and transpiration. About 186 cubic miles, or 762.6 cubic kilometers (75 percent of total precipitation) fall as precipitation over the oceans, and 24 cubic miles, or 98.4 cubic kilometers, are carried over land by the air from the oceans. About 62 cubic miles, or 254.2 cubic kilometers (25 percent) fall as precipitation over land. The 24 cubic miles carried from sea to land return to the sea via rivers.

At the temperatures and atmospheric pressures prevailing over the surface of the Earth, water can exist in all three of its phases: solid, liquid, or gas. Quite often, all three are present in the same place at the same time. Over a partly frozen lake or at the edge of the polar sea ice, the solid (ice) floats on top of the liquid (water), and in the air above there is the gas (water vapor). Our weather results from the constant changes of phase, between solid, liquid, and gas, and the transport of liquid water by rivers and ocean currents and of water vapor by air movements. Earth is the only planet in the solar system where water can exist as a liquid. On some of the outer planets and their satellites, such as the moons of Jupiter, water is abundant, but only as ice. Mars has water, but it is beneath the surface, and the atmospheric pressure is so low that any ice that melted would vaporize instantly. Venus is much too hot for water to exist except as a gas.

Heat pure water to about 212° F (100° C) and it will vaporize rapidly. We call this "boiling," and it occurs at 212° F only if the atmospheric pressure is at the sea-level average of 1013.25 millibars (= 29.9 inches [75.9 centimeters] of mercury = 14.7 pounds [6.6 kilograms] per square inch [6.5 square centimeters]; 1,000 millibars [mb] = 1 bar). Reduce the pressure and water boils at a lower temperature. Tibetans like to drink their tea while it is boiling, but they live above 12,000 feet (3.6 kilometers), where the average air pressure is around 660 millibars and water boils at about 190° F (88° C). Increase the atmospheric pressure and the boiling temperature rises.

At the surface between water and air, water molecules are constantly escaping into the air and returning to the body of water. This produces a very thin layer of water vapor mixed with air. Whether molecules can escape from this layer into the air beyond depends partly on the force with which the air presses down on the water surface. The air pressure over a particular area, such as 1 square inch (6.5 square centimeters), is the weight of all the air above that area. At sea level this amounts to 14.7 pounds (6.6 kilograms). The lower the pressure, the more readily water molecules escape into the air.

The ease with which water molecules can escape also depends on the concentration of water vapor already present in the air, because there is a limit to the amount of water vapor air can hold. When this limit is reached, the air is saturated and no more can enter. If the limit is exceeded, some of the vapor condenses into liquid. The amount of water vapor air can hold varies according to the air temperature. Warm air can hold more than cool air. The amount of water present in air as a proportion of the amount needed to saturate the air is called the "relative humidity" (RH). It is given as a percentage and varies with temperature. The amount of water vapor needed to saturate air (100 percent RH) at 40° F (4.4° C), for example, produces an RH of only 24 percent in air at 60° F (15.5°C).

Provided the air is not saturated, water will evaporate into it from all exposed water surfaces. As figure 2 shows, water evaporates from the oceans and lakes, and also from the ground when it is wet.

Water also evaporates from plant leaves, even when they are dry. Plants absorb water through their roots and use it both to transport the mineral nutrients they need from the ground to their cells, and to make their cells rigid. Water flows through plants constantly; when it reaches their leaves, it evaporates through pores in the surface. This is called "transpiration," and it adds to the water evaporating into the air.

Water vapor then mixes with the air and moves with it. Air over the ocean may drift across land, taking its moisture with it, and dry air over land may drift over the ocean, where water evaporates into it. Some of the water vapor is carried upward. Air temperature decreases with height, so RH increases with height. If the air contains enough water vapor, at a certain height it will condense into droplets and form clouds. The cloud base is at the height where water vapor starts to condense.

Cloud droplets are so small they fall only slowly, and those which fall from the bottom of the cloud evaporate again in the drier air below the cloud base. Droplets move up as well as down, carried in vertical air currents. Most of them reach heights at which the temperature is below freezing, and become ice crystals. These tend to cling to one another, forming snowflakes, but as they descend again they may enter warmer air where they melt. Most rain is snow that melted on its way down, even in the middle of summer. As they fall, droplets collide, which can cause them to join together, like the droplets that run down a windowpane, until they are large enough to fall all the way to the ground before they evaporate completely. If the air temperature throughout the cloud and beneath it is below freezing, of course, the snowflakes will not melt.

How the land drains

Watch rain falling onto the ground and you will see that the water soon disappears. Puddles may form, but they seldom last for long. When the rain stops, the ground dries.

Some of the water flows across the surface. How much travels this way depends on the intensity of the rainfall and how long it continues, the slope of the ground, and the condition of the surface. Buildings and city streets have hard, impermeable surfaces. All water falling on them runs down into drains that carry it away.

Under certain conditions water will also run over the surface of soil. This will happen when rain falls faster than water can soak into the soil, and when heavy rain batters the surface of the soil so tiny soil particles fill all the open spaces, forming a cap that water cannot penetrate.

Plants protect the soil surface. Much of the rain that falls on them evaporates directly and does not reach the ground at all. After a shower, the ground beneath shrubs is often as dry as it was before the rain. Water that falls to the ground does so slowly, dripping gently from plants rather than striking the surface directly. This makes a large difference. Really heavy rain—during a thunderstorm, for example—falls with considerable force. Droplets are traveling at about 20 MPH (32 KPH), and 2 inches (5.08 centimeters) of rain strike every square yard (0.84 square meter) of ground with a force of more than 1,200 foot-pounds (1,200 foot-pounds = 1,627 joules; a foot-pound is the force needed to move a mass of 1 pound [.45 kilogram] 1 foot [30 centimeters]). Water rarely flows across the surface of ground covered by vegetation, but often does so across bare ground. Heavy rain on a bare hillside is likely to flow immediately into the valley below, carrying a large amount of soil with it. Clearing plants—often trees—from hillsides has led to many floods, as well as serious soil erosion (see page 85).

Ordinarily, rain soaks into the ground. Soil is made of particles derived originally from rock, mixed with decaying plant and animal material. Dead leaves and twigs, the roots of dead plants, animal wastes, and the bodies of animals that have died all contribute to this material and form part of the soil, along with the vast numbers of small animals, fungi, and bacteria that feed on it.

Particles pack together, but there are always spaces between them. The number of spaces and their size depend on the size and shape of the particles. Clay particles pack together very tightly, with few spaces between them, because the particles are flat and stack on top of each other in overlapping patterns. They are also very small, less than 4 μm in diameter (1 μm = 0.00004 inch [0.001 millimeter]); 5,000 clay particles, laid side by side, would measure 1 inch (2.54 centimeters). Sand grains are 62.5–2000 μm across (0.002–0.08 inch, or .005–.2 centimeter). Since they are much bigger than clay particles, there is more space between them.

When soil is dry, the spaces between particles are filled with air. As water soaks downward, sinking under the force of gravity, it flows through these spaces, which are then filled with water. The more air space there is to start with, the faster the water will flow. You can easily measure the rate at which water flows through particles of different sizes. Experiment 27 in volume 6 suggests comparing the rate of flow through marbles and sand.

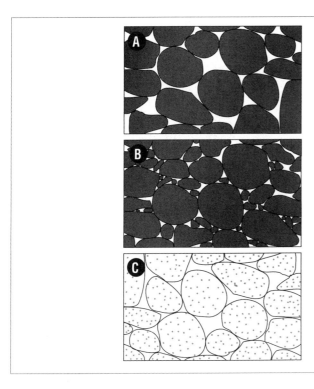

Figure 3: *Soil particles and porosity*
A. Large particles. Water passes easily.
B. Large particles with smaller particles among them. Water particles do not flow easily.
C. Large particles that are themselves porous. Water passes easily and is also absorbed.

As figure 3 shows, however, soils are not always composed of particles all of the same type and size. Diagram A shows a soil composed of large particles with large spaces through which water flows rapidly. In diagram B most of the spaces are filled by much smaller particles, which impede the flow of water. The particles in diagram C are large and also porous, so they absorb water. Water flows easily through a soil of this kind, and because the particles retain the water they absorb, the soil remains moist. After the water drains from the spaces between particles, the particles start releasing the water they have absorbed. This provides a continuing supply of water to plant roots.

Eventually all the spaces between particles fill with water. The soil is then said to be at its "field capacity." It can hold no more water, but drainage continues as water arrives from above. The water flows down further until it reaches a layer of impermeable material. This may be the solid rock lying beneath the soil, or a bed of tightly compacted clay. Water cannot penetrate it, so it accumulates above it.

Above the impermeable layer there is now a layer of soil that is completely saturated with water. Water fills all the spaces between its particles. Such a layer lies below all soils, even in deserts, although it may be a very long way below the surface. The water it contains is known as "groundwater." Layers of rock or other impermeable material are rarely horizontal, so the groundwater flows downhill. It flows very slowly because it is moving between and around soil particles. Its speed depends on the structure of the soil through which it moves. Fast-flowing groundwater might travel a few feet in a day, but through denser material or down a shallower gradient it might move only a few feet in a month.

The soil above the saturated layer is not permanently saturated; the boundary between the two layers is called the "water table." It marks the upper surface of the groundwater, but it is not like the surface of a river or lake because all the water is held between soil particles and the surface is not clearly defined.

As figure 4 illustrates, rainwater moves downward through the upper soil (arrows pointing downward) and continues to do so until this layer reaches its field capacity. Then water drains further and joins the groundwater in the saturated layer. If the rain continues, more and more water will accumulate in the saturated layer. The horizontal flow of groundwater is slow, and cannot remove water fast enough to prevent the water table from rising as the saturated layer thickens. As the water table nears the surface, the upper soil layer becomes waterlogged. Then hollows fill with water that cannot drain away, and water lies on the surface of level ground. This is one type of flooding.

Figure 4: *Water below ground.*

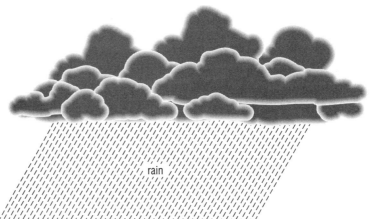

rain

unsaturated layer

water table

capillary fringe

ground waterflow

impermeable material

After the rain stops, the soil starts to dry. Water evaporates from the wet soil at the surface, which draws more water from below to fill the spaces between particles; this water also evaporates. Eventually, the upper, unsaturated soil layer is fairly dry, and many of the spaces between particles are filled with air. Then water starts moving upward from the water table through the "capillary fringe" (arrows pointing upward), a layer just a few inches thick.

"Capillarity" or "capillary motion" is the upward movement of water through a very narrow opening. It is what happens when blotting paper soaks up spilled ink. In liquid water, the molecules are attracted to one another and any individual molecule is attracted by others all around it, so the attractive force is equal in all directions. Molecules at the surface are not attracted equally in all directions, however, because there are no molecules above them. The force on the surface molecules holds them to the molecules on either side and below them. This causes a "surface tension," with the surface molecules held so firmly in place that they will support the weight of some insects, such as pond skaters (also known as "water striders").

An undisturbed large body of water, such as a puddle or pond, has a flat surface, because gravity is the strongest force acting on it. In a small volume, however, such as a single drop, surface tension pulls the water surface into the shape that requires the least energy to maintain: a sphere, which has the least surface area in relation to its volume. Another attractive force acts between the electric charge on water molecules (positive at the hydrogen end of the molecule and negative at the oxygen end) and opposite charge on molecules at the surface of a solid.

Figure 5 illustrates what happens to water in a very narrow tube. Molecules are attracted to the sides of the tube; some of them are drawn up it. This gives the surface a concave shape (diagram A). Surface tension then restores the more economical spherical shape

Figure 5: *Capillarity.*

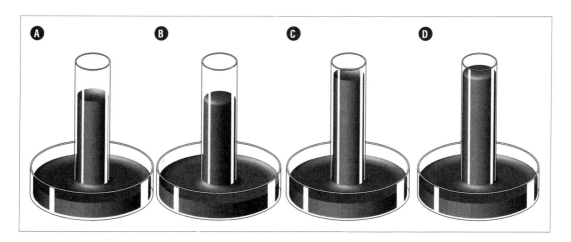

(diagram B), making the surface bulge upward in a convex shape. Now water molecules can move higher up the sides of the tube (diagram C), making the surface once more concave, and surface tension restores the convex shape (diagram D). Water will climb up a narrow tube in this way until its own weight prevents it from climbing higher. In soil, the tiny spaces between particles are like narrow tubes, but they are not all vertical. Water climbs up them by capillarity, but can travel further, because where the "tube" is not vertical it supports part of the weight of the water.

Above the capillary fringe, the soil continues to dry until more rain falls, but below the fringe, the groundwater continues to flow slowly downhill. The movement of water through the soil carries away the rain, but only if the soil is protected by plants so it can perform this function efficiently, and continuous heavy rain does not overwhelm its drainage capacity.

Rivers

Deep below ground, water that has drained from the surface moves slowly downhill. All continents and islands stand above sea level, although some areas within them may be lower, which means water flowing downhill must eventually reach this lowest possible level. Once such a basin has filled, water will overflow its rim and resume its downward progress. Gravity ensures that water must drain from the land into the sea.

Water drains in one direction down one side of a hill, and in another direction down the other side. This hill is usually one of a range of hills or mountains; the tops of these hills or mountains mark a boundary for the water draining from them, rather like the ridge of a roof. This boundary is called a "divide," because it is where the flow of water divides, some going one way and some the other. (In Britain, a divide is often called a "watershed," since it is the place from which water is shed.)

Rain does not fall only on the divide, of course. As water flows down from the divide, more joins it from the side of the slope. Eventually, the water reaches low ground, but beyond that more hills may rise, and water also drains from them. The entire area from which all the water drains into a particular low-lying area forms a "drainage basin." This is often known in North America as a "watershed" and in Britain as a "catchment."

As it flows down the side of the watershed, with more joining it all the time, the volume of groundwater increases and the water table rises until in some places it reaches the surface. After that it flows over the surface, finding its way around boulders and other obstructions along the lowest ground. The water has become a stream, small at first but growing larger as more and more water drains into it down the sides of the channel it makes for itself by washing away soft rock, small stones, and loose soil. At the bottom of the watershed many small rivers combine into a single, larger river that continues eventually to the sea.

Drainage basins can be very large and rivers long. In the United States, the Mississippi and Missouri rivers, which join to form a single river system, drain a basin of 1,243,700 square miles (3,233,620 square kilometers), extending from the Rockies in the west, the Canadian border in the north, and via the Ohio River, which flows into the Mississippi, to Pennsylvania in the east. The overall length of the Mississippi and Missouri rivers is 3,860 miles (6,176 kilometers). This is the third largest drainage basin in the world; averaged over the year, every second it discharges 620,000 cubic feet (16,740 cubic meters) of water into the Gulf of Mexico. The largest drainage basin is that of the Amazon, covering 2,722,000 square miles (7,077,200 square kilometers); the river, 4,000 miles (6,400 kilometers) long, discharges 4,200,000 cubic feet (113,400 cubic meters) of water into the Atlantic Ocean every second. The Congo, 2,716 miles (4,346 kilometers) long, drains 1,425,000 square miles (3,705,000 square kilometers) and discharges 1,400,000 cubic feet (37,800 cubic meters) of water per second into the Atlantic. Every continent has rivers of comparable length, the longest of all being the Nile, 4,157 miles (6,651 kilometers) from its source to its mouth on the southern shore of the Mediterranean Sea.

Always following the steepest gradient, over thousands of years rivers carry away material from their sides and bed, carving permanent channels. The force of gravity makes rivers flow and the steeper the slope the faster their waters move, but water is slowed by friction with the riverbed. The deeper the river, the faster it can flow, because the effect of friction is reduced, but no river can flow faster than about 20 MPH (32 KPH). Even so, the force of moving water is considerable. Kinetic energy, which is the energy of a body that is in motion, is proportional to the mass of the body and the square of its speed (see box on page 14); 1 U.S. gallon (3.8 liters) of (pure) water weighs 8.3 pounds (3.7 kilograms). Stand waist-deep in water flowing at 10 MPH (16 KPH), and the water will push against you with a force of about 23 pounds (10.4 kilograms). If the speed of the river increased slightly, to 12 MPH, that force would increase to 32 pounds (14.4 kilograms).

As long as the flow remains constant, rivers cope well enough with the water they transport, but the flow does not always remain constant. Where the upper parts of the watershed lie in mountains above the winter snowline, the spring thaw sends a surge of water into the drainage system. If the snowfall was heavier than usual,

Kinetic energy

Kinetic energy (KE), the energy of motion, is equal to half the mass of a moving body multiplied by the square of its velocity (or speed). Expressed algebraically, $KE = \frac{1}{2}mv^2$.

This formula gives a result in joules if m is in kilograms and v is in meters per second. If you need to calculate the force in pounds exerted by a mass measured in pounds moving in miles per hour, the formula must be modified slightly to $KE = mv^2 \div 2g$, where v is converted to feet per second (feet per second = miles per hour x 5,280 ÷ 3,600) and g is 32 (the acceleration due to gravity in feet per second).

that surge can be big enough to make rivers overflow their banks down in the valleys, far from the mountains. This effect can be predicted by calculating the "snow coefficient." This is the average depth of snow throughout the watershed, measured as a depth of liquid water (roughly one-tenth of the snow's thickness) divided by the total annual precipitation.

Seasonal fluctuations in rainfall also alter the amount of water carried by rivers. Whether the flow increases in winter or summer depends on the type of climate in the drainage basin. Heavier summer rainfall is typical of continental climates, heavier winter rainfall of maritime climates. You can tell which climates are continental, and which are maritime, by dividing the total annual rainfall into two parts, for the summer (April to September, in the northern hemisphere) and winter (October to March) periods and dividing the summer rainfall by the winter rainfall. If the result is more than 1, the climate is continental; if it is less than 1, it is maritime. For Kansas City the value is 2.2, indicating a strongly continental climate; for Seattle, it is 0.3, indicating a maritime climate; and for New York City, it is 1.0, indicating a climate between the two.

This has a dramatic effect on river flow. The Seine, flowing through Paris and draining a region of France with a maritime climate, carries almost four times more water in February than it does in August. The seasonal variation in flow increases greatly if the river also carries meltwater. In the Missouri River, meltwater from the Rockies, beginning in spring on the lower slopes and continuing into summer as the thaw reaches higher altitudes, joins summer rainwater as the river crosses the prairies. At the time of its lowest flow, the Missouri carries 4,200 cubic feet (113.4 cubic meters) of water per second, but at the time of its highest flow it carries 900,000 cubic feet (24,300 cubic meters) per second.

Monsoons bring the most extreme seasonal changes. Parts of Africa and North America experience monsoons, but they are most marked in southern Asia. There are two monsoons (*monsoon* is from an Arabic word meaning "season"). The winter monsoon brings hot, dry winds, and the summer monsoon brings heavy rain. Seoul, South Korea, has an average annual rainfall of 49.2 inches (125 centimeters), but 25.3 inches (64.3 centimeters) of it fall in July and August, the two monsoon months, and if the rains are unusually heavy, flooding is likely.

This happened in July 1996, when 21 inches (53.3 centimeters) of rain fell in just three days along the border between North and South Korea. Two towns, Yonchon and Munsan, were almost completely submerged, sending 50,000 people fleeing onto higher ground, and mudslides triggered by the rains killed more than 40 people. The same monsoon rains also caused the Ganges and Brahmaputra rivers to overflow, damaging or destroying the homes of nearly 5 million people in Bangladesh. By mid-July, 60 villages had been inundated in Assam, India, and 120 camps had to be set up to accommodate 1.5 million people displaced from their homes.

In China, the flooding started in late June 1996; by July 8, the floodwaters were 20 feet (600 centimeters) deep in parts of the provinces of Zhejiang, south of Shanghai, and Hunan, in southeastern China. Those floods killed more than 1,500 people, injured or damaged the property of 20 million people, and destroyed at least 2.5 million acres (4 million hectares) of crops. Approximately 8 million soldiers and civilians were mobilized to conduct rescue operations and strengthen the dikes and flood walls along the banks of the Yangtze. The Chinese government estimated the damage caused by the floods cost about $12 billion.

When a large river is severely overloaded, the effects are felt in its tributaries. Water can flow with great force, which is sometimes sufficient to push back the water flowing in tributaries, causing them to overflow as well.

It is not only monsoon climates that make rivers burst their banks. Heavy storms can make this happen anywhere. While Asia suffered torrential monsoons, in southern Québec 11 inches (28 centimeters) of rain fell in two days in July, and about 200 miles (320 kilometers) north of Montréal, the Saguenay River and its tributaries burst their banks. Tents had to be used as emergency shelters for about 3,000 of the 12,000 people evacuated from La Baie and not allowed to return for fear that dams might burst, inundating the town (two tents were also provided for cats and dogs). Italy also suffered, when storms caused flooding in the area around Lake Maggiore on July 7 and 8.

Water flows along the easiest route, wearing away soft material and skirting tougher rocks. That is how river channels form; their size is determined by the volume of water they usually carry. A sudden, large increase in that volume causes flooding, but the underlying principle holds firm. Water flows downhill, along the easiest route, even if that route sometimes takes it across fields, along streets, and through homes. Floods are entirely natural, but no less destructive for that.

Floodplains and meanders

Water always flows downhill. The steeper the hill, the faster it flows and the faster it flows, the more energy it possesses. This energy is called the "hydraulic head" of the river, and it is proportional to the mass of water and its height, or its "elevation potential energy."

Potential energy is the energy a body possesses by virtue of its location. Any object has potential energy if it is raised above a surface to which it may later fall. A book on a shelf has potential energy. If someone knocks it down, it will fall to the floor. Its motion, from shelf to floor, converts its potential energy into kinetic energy (energy of motion), and its kinetic energy is transferred to the floor when it lands. The floor absorbs the energy and becomes warmer, but by an amount too small to measure.

Rivers do not fall directly, like books dropping from shelves. Their journey is more like the one you experience when you ride downhill on a bike. Start at the top, with just enough push to set you rolling, and your speed by the time you reach the bottom depends on how long and steep the hill is. In the same way, if you want to know how fast a river will flow, you need one more item of information in addition to the mass of the water. You need to know how far the water travels horizontally while it descends vertically. In fact, you need to know the gradient of the riverbed.

High in the mountains, where most rivers begin, gradients are usually steep. The water falls a long way down the mountainside while traveling only a short distance horizontally. Consequently, the water has a great deal of energy. There is not much water, however, and mountains are made from rocks that are not easily worn away, so although the river may be a torrent, it cuts only a narrow channel between hard rocks.

By the time it reaches the plains, far from the mountains, the river carries much more water, because of the many smaller rivers that have joined it as tributaries along its route. Here, though, the gradient is much shallower. The river travels a long way horizontally for only a small vertical drop. It slows and, because of its additional volume of water, its channel widens.

Where the gradient is very shallow, so the water hardly descends at all as it moves forward, and the river is not contained between banks made from hard rock, eddies may influence its course. Small irregularities in the bank or bed start water swirling, so it does not flow smoothly. Watch any river and you will see eddies and even little whirlpools. This type of flow is called "turbulent"; smooth flow, where all the water is flowing in the same direction at the same speed, is called "laminar."

Turbulent flow can cause a slow-moving river to follow a very curving path. There is a river in western Turkey called the Menderes, which twists and turns many times as it approaches the Aegean Sea, into which it discharges its waters. In some places its curves are so extreme the river actually turns back on itself and almost describes a circle. Menderes is its modern name, but the ancient Greeks knew it as the Maiandros, from which the Romans derived the word *maeander* to describe this kind of twisting and turning river course. From *maeander* comes our word *meander*.

A meandering river flows over soil rather than hard rock. It also carries soil, as silt and particles of various sizes that have washed into it and its tributaries further upstream. Because it flows slowly, the water has less energy than it had when it flowed over steeper gradients, and some of this suspended material falls to its bed. Accumulating steadily over thousands of years, this raises the bed, making the river shallower and, therefore, wider.

When water flows along a curved path, however, not all the water flows at the same speed. The water on the outside of the

Figure 6: *In Mineral County, Colorado, the San Juan River meanders west of Wolf Creek Pass.* (W. B. Hamilton and U.S. Geological Survey)

curve has farther to travel than water on the inside of the curve, so it flows faster. Flowing faster, it has more energy and can carry more suspended material. It erodes the bank against which it flows, but not by battering it. That would press soil particles closer together and strengthen the bank. Rather, it pulls particles out from the bank and carries them downstream. This is an example of the behavior of any liquid or gas flowing through a constriction, which was discovered more than two centuries ago by Daniel Bernoulli (see box below).

Material is eroded from the bank on the outside of each bend, so the bend itself moves outward. At the same time, because the water on the inside of the bend moves more slowly and has less energy, some of the suspended material it carries is deposited there. As figure 7 shows, the bends tend to become more extreme.

There is also a second effect. Once the pattern of meanders is established, continuing erosion on one side and sedimentation on the other moves the entire system of meanders forward. The pattern remains more or less the same, but it advances.

The land over which it advances is then a floodplain, bounded by the extreme limits of the widest meander. The floodplain is covered with fine-grained soil deposited by the river and through which the river continues to cut its channel. Soil transported by rivers is called "alluvium," and on floodplains the upper layers of soil are alluvial. Ordinarily, soil is composed of mineral particles derived from the underlying rock, but alluvial soils are unrelated to the rock beneath them. They have been carried to their present location. Alluvial soils are often very fertile, which combined with

The Bernoulli effect

In 1738, the Swiss mathematician Daniel Bernoulli (1700–82) published a book called *Hydrodynamica*, in which he showed that when the speed at which a fluid (liquid or gas) flows increases, the pressure within the flow decreases. He reached this conclusion while studying water flowing through a pipe from a tank where the water level was high to another where it was lower. In the end, of course, the water level was the same in both tanks, but while the water was flowing Bernoulli found the pressure within the flowing stream was related to the speed with which it flowed. This is summarized as $p + \frac{1}{2}rV^2 = $ a constant, where p is the pressure, r the density of the fluid, and V its velocity (speed).

If, for example, the fluid flows through a tube with a constriction in it, assuming the fluid is not compressed, the rate of flow must increase at the constriction, because the same volume of fluid must pass through there in a given time as passes through every other point in the tube. It follows from Bernoulli's equation that the pressure must decrease at the constriction. Although this sounds unlikely, performing experiments 6, 7, 8, and 9 in volume 6 should convince you.

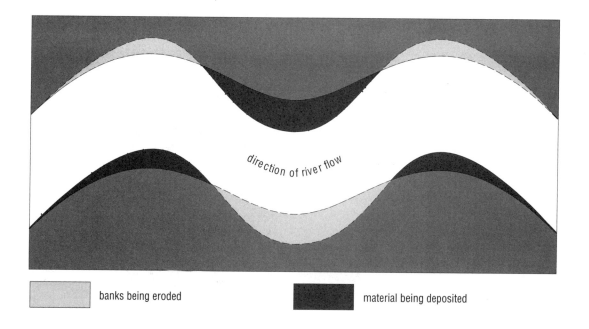

direction of river flow

banks being eroded   material being deposited

the level surface of the plain, makes them attractive to farmers. Floodplains are often intensively farmed and densely populated.

Unfortunately, a floodplain is a dangerous place to live. Although the meander system advances only slowly, and there is plenty of time to adjust to the changing position of the river, "floodplain" has a second meaning. Meandering rivers are shallow, because of the large amount of material they deposit on their beds, and a sudden surge of water from upstream will make them overflow their banks. Floodplains can experience sudden floods that destroy crops and homes. In Bangladesh, where most of the country is low-lying, such flooding is common and usually catastrophic.

Drawing A in figure 8 shows a floodplain of this type. The main river flows across a level valley with high ground to either side. Smaller rivers, flowing along channels cut through the high ground, join it as tributaries; some of these have produced smaller floodplains of their own. As you see, the width of the floodplain is determined by the widest meanders.

This is only one kind of floodplain. Drawing B shows a river much like the Mississippi. It meanders so slowly across so wide a plain that parts of meanders have been isolated from the main flow. When a meander becomes so extreme that there is only a short distance between the two sides of the loop, the river may cut a new channel across the meander, leaving the old loop isolated as an oxbow lake. The river may also divide into two or more channels that diverge and rejoin in a braided pattern.

Figure 7: How meanders form a floodplain.

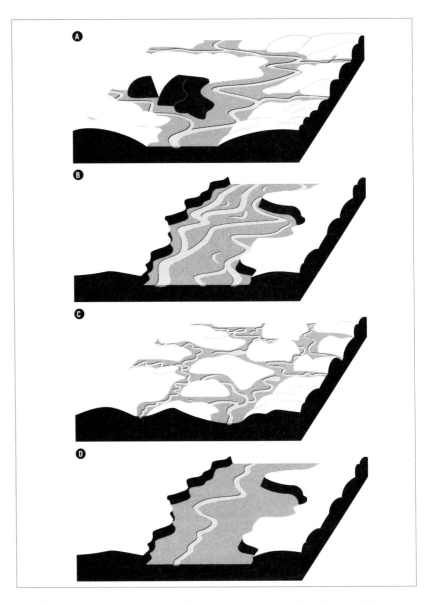

Figure 8: *River meanders.*

There are places where the ground is very broken, with many humps. This kind of landscape, shown in drawing C, is most often found where glaciers have retreated, leaving behind a moraine of boulders and gravel, all heaped up in mounds. Here, the river divides repeatedly, weaving around the humps with many channels, each of which produces its own small floodplain.

Although meander patterns often remain fairly constant for a long time, they can also change dramatically. This can result in a river with meanders apparently much too small for the floodplain they have made, as shown in drawing D. In fact, though, the changing course of the river has carried the meanders first to one side of the plain and then the other.

Regardless of its precise pattern, a meandering river is not to be trusted. The fertile soil it deposits across the even surface of its floodplain tempts farming communities, but the river may overflow its banks with little warning, inundating fields and homes. Such flooding is entirely natural. It allows the river to release excess water onto surrounding land, from which it can drain. This makes it difficult, and sometimes hazardous, to prevent flooding on floodplains (see page 104), and some scientists believe the only way to prevent flood damage is to advise people not to settle in such places.

Aquifers, springs, and wells

Slowly, the water below ground flows downhill, inching its way through the porous soil or rock. The water itself is called "groundwater." The material through which it flows is an "aquifer." Not all rocks will allow water to flow, even though they may be fully saturated. A rock that prevents or seriously restricts the flow of water through it, despite being saturated, is called an "aquiclude" or "aquifuge"; if an aquifer meets an aquiclude, the passage of groundwater will be halted at the boundary. As it accumulates, the water table will rise and groundwater flow will resume above the aquiclude. The aquifer then lies above an aquiclude and is said to be "perched."

The difference between an aquifer and an aquiclude arises from the size of the pore spaces between particles. Where the pore spaces are large, water flows easily, but where they are small, water moves by capillarity. In the capillary fringe, above the water table, capillarity, the movement of water against gravity through very small spaces, draws water upward (see page 11), but it also ensures the pores remain filled with water, which impedes horizontal flow. Water molecules are attracted to the sides of the pores with a force greater than that of gravity. Clay, composed of minute particles, can become saturated with water and yet severely impede the movement of groundwater.

If the pore spaces are too large to allow water to be affected by capillarity, the rate at which water flows through them is proportional to the fourth power of the radius of the spaces. Take two glass tubes, for example, one with a radius double ($2\times$) that of the other, and water will flow through the larger tube 16 times (2^4) faster than through the narrow one.

The rate at which water will move through a particular type of material is a measure of the permeability, also called the "hydraulic conductivity," of that material; the permeability of different soil materials is classified as slow, moderate, or rapid. The table shows what these classifications mean in terms of the speed with which groundwater moves.

CLASSIFICATION OF SOIL PERMEABILITY

Class	Permeability (inches per hour)
Slow	
very slow	less than 0.05 (less than .13 cm)
slow	0.05–0.20 (.13–.59 cm)
Moderate	
moderately slow	0.20–0.80 (.59–2.03 cm)
moderate	0.80–2.50 (2.03–6.35 cm)
moderately rapid	2.50–5.00 (6.35–12.7 cm)
Rapid	
rapid	5.00–10.00 (12.7–25.4 cm)
very rapid	more than 10.00 (more than 25.4 cm)

Prolonged, heavy rain usually brings no immediate change to a river. If the land on either side is cultivated, you may see pipes discharging water from fields where farmers have installed underground drainage systems for the purpose, but you will see little or no water flowing across the surface and spilling over the banks. The river continues to flow as before, and the water level does not begin to rise until some time has elapsed. It is not until hours or even days later, when the rain may have ceased, that the river starts rising and there is a risk of flooding. The reason, of course, is that the river is fed not by surface flow and drainage from fields, but by underground aquifers. Water draining into the aquifer over the whole drainage basin, or the part of it experiencing the heavy rain, increases the thickness of the saturated layer, but it takes time for the additional water to reach the river. How long it takes depends on the distance it must travel, the permeability of the aquifer, and the gradient.

As the drawing A in figure 9 shows, rivers flow where the ground surface lies below the water table. When heavy rain increases the content of the aquifer, water enters the river from below the water table, not from above it. If the material composing the aquifer is the same over a large area, so water flows through all of it at the

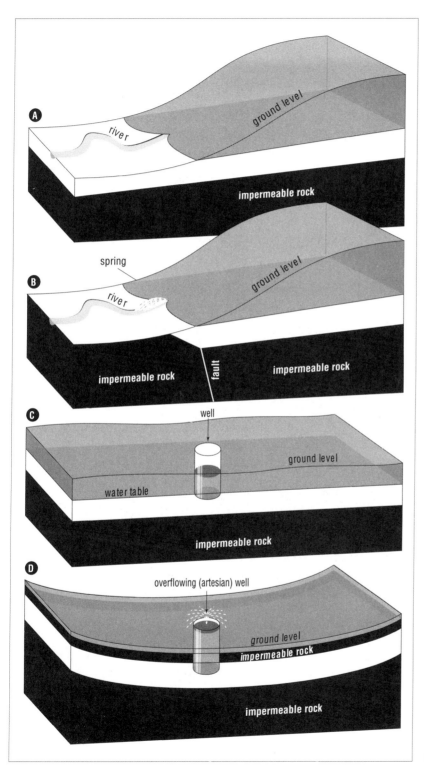

Figure 9: *Groundwater, rivers, springs, and wells.*

same rate, the water level will rise simultaneously along an entire stretch of the river.

Suppose, though, that the aquifer meets an obstruction. Perhaps the composition of the soil changes, with sand giving way to clay, for example, forming an aquiclude. Or the rock of the underlying impermeable layer may be faulted, so part of it has been raised or lowered and the aquifer meets an impermeable wall. Water will accumulate, the water table will rise, and then the flow will resume over the top of the obstruction.

It may be, however, that the higher water table lies at or very close to the ground surface, as in drawing B of figure 9. In this case, groundwater will flow over the surface. Depending on the type of surface, water may fill a small pool or soak into a patch of adjacent ground, making it permanently muddy. In either case it will then overflow. If the ground surface remains below the level of the water table, the spring will feed a small stream. If the ground rises again farther down the slope, water will soak back into the ground and rejoin the aquifer. The place where groundwater reaches the surface is a spring.

Springs can occur anywhere. They result from the formation of rock and soil below ground and, although all rivers start as springs in the uplands, springs can also be found in valleys and on the plains. Some are more dependable than others, but many have never been known to run dry, which means the aquifers feeding them are never seriously depleted.

Heavy rain or melting snow on higher ground can turn a gentle spring into a raging torrent. The spring marks the place where the water table reaches ground level. Should it rise even higher, because the addition of more water has increased the thickness of the saturated layer, water will pour freely over the surface. It no longer has to make its way slowly through porous rock or soil, so its rate of flow is determined only by gravity; the saturated layer will drain rapidly. What was a small stream then becomes a fast-flowing river, often dividing and rejoining as it courses down a hillside, and its water is delivered quickly to the larger river of which it is a tributary. This will raise the level of the main river much faster than water that travels all the way below ground.

If there is no river nearby, you need not hunt for a spring in order to find water. Almost certainly it lies beneath your feet, and you can reach it by digging a hole. As drawing C of figure 9 shows, it is a simple matter, at least in principle, to dig a hole from ground level down to below the water table. Do this and the bottom of the hole will fill with water you can extract with a bucket or pump. You have made a well. In practice, it may not be easy, because the water table may be at a considerable depth and digging a deep hole is always hard work.

An aquifer lying beneath permeable soil is said to be "unconfined." A "confined" aquifer flows between two layers of impermeable material. It might be, for example, that a layer of solid rock forms the base, and there is a layer of densely compacted clay above the saturated layer, sealing it from above. If the upper impermeable layer is covered by a deep layer of permeable soil, a second saturated layer may develop, producing two aquifers separated from one another by an impermeable layer. The lower aquifer is then confined and the upper one unconfined.

Layers of rock are often undulating, so they form depressions and domes. When groundwater flows into a depression in the underlying impermeable layer, it will accumulate there until the water table rises high enough for the flow to spill over the opposite edge. If the aquifer is confined, however, the water table cannot rise. The aquifer will become saturated, and then the weight of water flowing into it will exert enough pressure to force it over the opposite lip. In the situation illustrated by drawing D of figure 9, the aquifer is full and the pressure on the water in the depression increases toward the center, because of the weight of water pushing against it. If it were unconfined, the water level in the depression would rise until the water table was at the same height in the depression and to either side of it.

Drill a hole from the surface and through the upper impermeable layer, and this is what will happen: Once the pressure is released at one point, water will rise at that point. A well sunk into the lowest point in the depression will yield water without any need for buckets or pumps. The well will overflow, and if it pierces the depression at a level markedly lower than that of the impermeable rock to either side, as drawing D in figure 9, water will gush from it with some force. You can demonstrate this for yourself, using rubber or plastic tubing to represent the confining layers. Experiment 28 in voume 6 explains how to do it.

At Lillers, a small town not far from Lille in northern France, a well of this kind was dug in the year 1126. Lillers was then in the province of Artois (now the département of Pas de Calais). The Roman name for Artois was *Artesium*, which gave the French their adjective *artésien*, which in English becomes "artesian." Overflowing wells, which need no pumping because they tap into groundwater that is held under pressure, are often called "artesian wells."

If you live near a river in the plains or in a valley several miles wide, heavy rain need not worry you. It is not the rain falling on the plain or in the valley that will make the river flood, but rain falling over a large part of the area the river drains, or snow melting in the far-off mountains; the flood waters may travel many miles below ground before they emerge, possibly with little warning, to inundate fields and homes.

Vegetation and natural drainage

July and August are the rainy months in Nepal. That is when the Asian summer monsoon brings torrential downpours. The monsoon is not altogether reliable. In some years the rainfall is much higher than in others. In 1996 it was high.

Late on Monday, August 5, the rains triggered landslides that swept away dozens of homes in the village of Jhagraku, about 55 miles (88 kilometers) northeast of the capital, Katmandu. At least 40 people were killed, bringing to 218 the number of Nepalese people who had died in landslides and floods so far in 1996.

Nepal is a small country sandwiched between India and Tibet, in the Himalayas. It has some of the highest mountains in the world, including Everest, Kangchenjunga, and Annapurna, but also relatively low-lying, level ground at the foot of the mountains. Much of this area is cultivated, growing mainly rice. On higher ground farmers grow corn, millet, and other crops in terraced fields. At one time, the mountainsides were densely forested with pine and juniper, giving way to juniper shrubs and grassland at higher altitudes. Little by little, however, poor farmers were forced to extend the area of cultivated land farther up the slopes, clearing forest to make way for their fields and homes.

Then, in 1953, Sir Edmund Hillary and Sherpa Tensing climbed to the summit of Everest, and Nepal attracted the attention of the world just as it was seeking to develop its economy. Homes, hospitals, and schools were built, and roads and bridges for access to them, and then an airfield. The improved access brought tourists and climbers. They had to be accommodated and, in that mountain climate, they needed fuel for warmth and cooking. The fuel and building materials came from the forests. By the 1970s foreign visitors to the Everest region were arriving at the rate of 5,000 a year, and three times that number of Nepalese moved into the area to provide the services they needed. Most of the forest was cleared.

Today, with international aid to help, the Nepalese are planting forests to replace those which were lost in the 1970s, but the price of that clearance is still being paid. The villagers of Jhagraku are among those who are paying.

Each year, the monsoon rains flow almost unimpeded down the mountainsides. They carry with them soil washed from the surface (see page 85) that ends in the Ganges River. So much has been carried over the last quarter of a century that it has made new islands in the river. Before it reaches the Ganges, however, the mixture of mud and rock destroys everything in its path.

Nepal is far from unique. The mountains of Greece were once densely forested, but forest clearance was already well advanced by about 500 B.C., and people living in the lowlands had to endure the floods, landslides, and mudslides that resulted. In China the effects continue to this day. Between the Great Wall and the high, grassland plateau of Mongolia there is a plain formed by a deep, yellow soil called "loess," deposited by winds from central Asia. At one time this plain was forested, but between the 7th and 9th centuries A.D., the forest was cleared. Rains then began to wash the yellow soil into the river to which the loess gives its name, the Yellow River. As the soil settled on the riverbed, the river became shallower and overflowed its banks more often. It still causes catastrophic flooding. The Apennine Mountains, in Italy, were once forested. Roman troops were wary of them, because of the cover they afforded to enemy forces. As Florence expanded in the 12th century, the trees were felled to provide building material and were never replanted. The hillsides were left bare, and the Arno, carrying water draining from them, has repeatedly caused catastrophic floods since 1117, when the first was recorded (see page 1).

Plants greatly reduce the risk of flooding and mudslides. They do this in the first place by capturing water and returning it to the air before it can drain away. The process is called "transpiration," and it moves a surprisingly large amount of water. During the six months from the time its seed germinates until it releases its own seeds and dies, a sunflower plant may transpire more than 50 U.S. gallons (190 liters) of water. A birch tree may transpire 95 U.S. gallons (361 liters) of water a day, and an oak tree 180 U.S. gallons (684 liters). Indeed, trees are able to move so much water that species which grow naturally on riverbanks and in other wet places and can tolerate very moist soils are often grown to help dry out wet ground. Through the combined effects of transpiration and evaporation, a forest immediately returns to the air about 75 percent of the rain that falls on it. The precise amount varies according to the temperature and humidity of the air above the treetops.

Leaves and stems exposed to the rain are wetted. Some of the moisture evaporates from them, and some drips from leaf tips or runs down stems, to fall on leaves and stems at a lower level, from which more evaporates.

At the same time, water is constantly entering plant roots and moving through the plant. The water carries nutrients to each cell and, by filling the cells, gives them rigidity. Woody plants, such as trees and shrubs, have rigid stems and branches, but other plants, such as herbs and grasses, are able to stand erect only because of the water flowing through them. The water must continue to flow, which means it must leave the plant and be replaced by more water drawn from the soil. It passes through pores, called "stomata" in leaves and "lenticels" in roots, stems, and branches, and evaporates from the surface.

Sometimes, the amount of water entering the air from plant transpiration and the amount from evaporation from the soil and plant surfaces are measured together. This is simpler than measuring each separately, and the combined process is then known as "evapotranspiration."

Walk through a forest on a hot day and you will notice the air is cooler and more still than the air outside. It is also moister. The trees provide shade, of course, and shelter from the wind, which accounts for part of the difference, but transpiration also contributes. As transpired water evaporates, the latent heat of vaporization is taken from the plant surfaces and surrounding air, which has a cooling effect.

All this water moving into the air above a forest increases its humidity, so clouds tend to form. This is another climatic effect forests have. Altogether, a forest produces a climate different from that of the surrounding, unforested area.

It is not only forests that produce a local climate, called a "microclimate," different from that of their surroundings. All types of vegetation do so, including grasses. Of course, if you walk across grassland you will not be aware of this, because the microclimate does not extend beyond the top of the grass and most of your body is outside it. At ground level, however, the temperature, humidity, and wind are altered in just the same way as in a forest, although grasses transpire much less water than trees do, because the plants are smaller. By day, most plants transpire 0.6–10 ounces (1.68–28 grams) of water per hour from each square yard (0.84 square meter) of leaf surface, and by night about one-tenth of that.

If transpiration is the first line of defense plants provide against floods, their roots are the second. Roots penetrate the soil and actively search for water. In most plants, the roots first grow in length and later produce side roots, dividing into ever smaller branches, only when they find water. Like all living things, roots die and then decompose, but for a time the passages they have forced through the soil remain. These increase the amount of pore space in the soil, which allows surplus water to drain downward more easily and join the groundwater.

Roots are hidden below ground, so most of the time we are unaware of them. Try digging anywhere near trees, however, and you will soon see just how extensive they can be. Even then, unless you are able to dig a deep trench, which is difficult, you will find only those roots which are close to the surface, and you may not notice the smaller roots, because your spade will cut through them.

Most coniferous trees have fairly shallow roots. This makes them much more likely to be blown down by strong winds than broadleaved trees, such as oak and beech. When they are blown down their roots are exposed, but only a part of the whole root system, because the smaller roots break as the tree falls. Although the roots are not deep, they extend sideways farther than the branches above ground. Broad-leaved trees root more deeply, some of them producing conical taproots that grow vertically downward to a considerable depth. For most plants, the total mass of the root system is at least equal to the mass standing above ground. If you could stretch out all the roots and root hairs of a plant end to end, those of a tree would reach hundreds of miles and fill thousands of cubic feet of space. Even small plants often have huge root systems. The roots of a single wheat plant might extend more than 40 miles (64 kilometers) if they were all joined together in a single line, and those of a rye plant would reach about 50 miles (80 kilometers). A corn plant growing by itself, with no other plants to crowd it, will use its roots to "claim" more than 100 cubic yards (76.5 cubic meters) of soil. The roots of a fully grown wheat plant penetrate 6 feet (180 centimeters) or so beneath the surface, and some prairie grasses root even deeper, to 8 feet (240 centimeters) or more.

Roots allow air to penetrate the soil and, as they die, they leave vegetable matter to feed small animals and tunnels to help them move around. The animals, especially worms, then make more tunnels of their own, lining them with mucus that prevents them from collapsing. This, too, helps the soil to drain, but if there are no plants, there is no food for the animals, and they leave.

Remove all the vegetation and the situation soon begins to change. Transpiration and evaporation from plant surfaces cease immediately, and all of the rain falls to the ground and remains there, with only evaporation from the soil surface and natural drainage to remove it. Just above ground level the microclimate becomes warmer, because there are no longer plants to shade the surface and evapotranspiration to cool the air by removing latent heat. As the ground warms, the decomposition of dead plant material accelerates, because the chemical reactions by which soil organisms break down large, complex molecules into smaller, simpler ones work two to three times faster for every 18° F (10° C) increase in temperature. Decomposition ordinarily releases nutrients that are absorbed by the roots of living plants, but in the absence of plants the nutrients accumulate. For a time the soil becomes very fertile, but if there are no plants to take advantage of the nutrients, the situation does not last long. The nutrients are soluble; the rain washes them out of the soil. After a few years the soil has lost its fertility, and it is very difficult to grow plants in it.

Below ground, roots decay. The spaces they make fill with soil particles washed into them from above, and there are no new roots to maintain the amount of pore space. Worms and other animals die or leave, and their tunnels also fill. Gradually the soil loses its structure and becomes less permeable.

If the original vegetation was forest, felling and removing the trees scar the surface. Vehicles move among the trees, and timber is removed by dragging whole trunks across the ground. Small plants are destroyed, and the layer of soil beneath the surface layer is packed down by the weight of traffic over it. The routes along which logs have been hauled and those most used by vehicles are worn into gullies.

Heavy rain pounds the soil, churning it into mud. Water drains downward, but slowly and with difficulty because of the reduction in soil permeability. Before long, most of the surplus water flows directly over the surface and along the gullies, turning them into small rivers.

These problems can occur anywhere, but they are especially severe on high ground. This is because rainfall there is usually heavier than at lower levels. Air is forced to rise as it crosses high ground, and when it rises it cools, on average by 5.5° F (3° C) for every 1,000 feet (300 meters). Cool air can hold less water vapor than warm air can, so as it cools the rising air may become saturated. Suppose, for example, that at the bottom of a 2,000-foot (600-meter) hill the air is at about 70° F (21° C) and the relative humidity (RH) 40 percent (RH is the amount of water vapor present in the air as a percentage of the amount needed to saturate the air at that temperature). By the time the air has risen almost to the top of the hill, its temperature will have fallen to about 60° F (16° C) and its RH will be about 100 percent. Clouds will form and rainfall will be higher than at the lower level. As you know if you have ever been walking in the mountains, fog and rain are common there, even when the weather is dry down in the valleys. Caracas, Venezuela, lies 3,418 feet (1,043 meters) above sea level, and its annual rainfall is 33 inches (83.9 centimeters). Maracaibo, not far away and in the same latitude, is at an altitude of 20 feet (6 meters) and has about 23 inches (58.4 centimeters) of rain a year. The 10-inch (25.4-centimeter) difference results from the different altitudes of the two cities.

Rain in the hills falls onto sloping ground, often onto steep slopes. If the ground is bare and the soil has lost its permeability, water will flow directly over the surface, plunging into the valleys and quickly filling rivers. At the same time, because there are no longer plant roots to trap and hold soil particles, the soil washes into the rivers, settles on riverbeds, and further increases the likelihood of flooding.

This is why Florence, villages in Nepal, and the towns and villages along the floodplain of the Yellow River suffer such frequent floods, landslides, and mudslides. The forests that once cloaked the mountainsides and protected them, and many other towns and villages on every continent, have been removed, and the best way to reduce flooding would be to restore them. That is what the Nepalese are doing, but they recognized the problem before the soil had deteriorated to the point at which reforestation became difficult and required large fertilizer applications to compensate for the lost nutrients. Elsewhere, reforestation is much more expensive and uncertain. Even so, in the long run it is probably the most effective remedy.

Floods and agriculture

The Nile Floods and the Aswân Dam

Each year, when the star we call Sirius and the ancient Egyptians knew as Sothis appeared on the horizon, the river overflowed its banks. Sothis was the star of Isis, wife of Osiris and the goddess who was believed to have discovered wheat and barley. It was Isis who created and became all vegetation. She was the cultivated field itself, and when the reapers cut the first sheaves of the harvest they beat their breasts and called upon her, mourning the spirit their sickles had slain.

The river, of course, was the Nile, and unlike the Tigris and Euphrates, the two other great rivers of the ancient world, its floods were fairly dependable. The people of Mesopotamia, living between the Tigris and Euphrates, suffered sudden, violent flash floods (see page 90) that caused appalling destruction and strongly influenced their outlook on the world. Mesopotamian priests spent much of their time studying the sky and state of the rivers, and they developed many techniques aimed at divining what the waters were about to do. Politically, this need to be constantly alert to natural phenomena led to the emergence of strong governments and laws as well as the beginning of science. For the Egyptians, life was much more predictable. Their mainly peaceful and prosperous civilization flourished beside the banks of the Nile, in what was in effect a long, narrow oasis bordered by desert to east and west, and the way of life of ordinary people changed little for almost 3,000 years.

Apart from its many tributaries, two principal rivers combine to form the Nile. The White Nile, which is the longer, rises in Burundi; the Blue Nile, which carries the greater volume of water and was the main source of the annual flood, rises in the highlands of Ethiopia. They meet at Khartoum, the capital of Sudan, and about 200 miles (320 kilometers) farther downstream they are joined by the Atbara River. The Atbara and its tributaries are no more than strings of pools in the dry season, but in the rainy season the river is large and muddy, and an important source of the silt on which Egyptian farmers used to rely.

Egypt itself has a dry climate. Cairo has an average annual rainfall of barely more than 1 inch (2.54 centimeters), and Aswân, 555 miles (888 kilometers) to the south, rarely receives any rain at all. Further upstream, however, the rainfall increases, and the average over the highland sources of both the White and Blue Niles is about 50 inches (127 centimeters). The Nile's great size results from the huge area it drains—more than 1 million square miles (2.6 million square kilometers)—rather than a rainy climate in any large part of its basin.

Over part of the Nile's basin, in Sudan and Ethiopia, the rainfall is strongly seasonal, peaking in July and August. This sends a surge of water into the river, which reaches its maximum flow in Egypt in late August and early September, when the river would flood.

North of Aswân, the annual floods formed a floodplain covered by a layer of rich, alluvial (river-borne) soil, more than 60 feet (18 meters) thick near the coast. Each year the flood brought an additional 110–160 million tons (121–176 million tonnes) of silt. Some settled on the land to replenish it, and the rest was carried into the sea. In fact, the Nile is not exceptionally muddy. During the flood the water carried an average of about 1,600 parts of silt to 1 million parts of water, which is less than that in the Colorado and Missouri rivers. This floodplain, nowhere more than 12 miles (19.2 kilometers) wide, opens north of Cairo into a delta, which extends 100 miles (160 kilometers) to the Mediterranean and reaches a maximum width of 155 miles (248 kilometers). The floodplain and delta provide the farmland.

Traditionally, embankments running from the river to the edge of the desert divided the land to the south of the delta into basins, ranging in size from 2,000 to more than 80,000 acres (800 to more than 32,000 hectares). Short canals led from the river to the basins and were sealed by dikes that were not opened until the river was in flood.

Farmers had advance warning of the flood, because regular readings were taken of the water level at various points upstream by means of "Nilometers." The most accurate of these was located at Roda Island, in Cairo. Figure 10 shows how it worked. River water was fed along a tunnel into a cistern. Because water finds its own level, the level in the cistern was always the same as that in the river, but it could be read more easily. In this example the water level is read from a graduated obelisk in the center of the cistern. Other Nilometers used graduations on the side of the cistern itself. The most complete surviving series of Nilometer records, from Roda, covers most years from A.D. 622 to 1522.

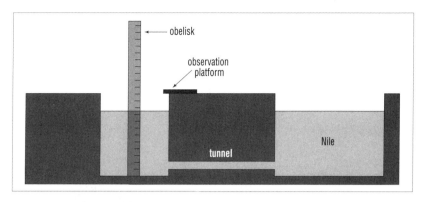

obelisk

observation platform

Nile

tunnel

Figure 10: *Nilometer.*

When word came that the river was rising, muddy water was allowed to flow along the canals and covered the basins to a depth of several feet. The water remained there for several weeks, during which the mud settled and the water soaked into the ground. Then, as the river fell, surplus water drained back into it, leaving behind its soft, sticky mud in which the farmers planted their seeds. Once the river level had fallen, any additional irrigation the crops needed had to be supplied by water lifted from wells, and when the mud dried it became very hard.

This system must have come close to what people mean nowadays when they talk of "sustainable farming." It produced one crop a year, but it did so year after year for thousands of years, with no sign of the soil deteriorating. Unfortunately, it had one drawback. The Nile flood was never completely reliable. Sometimes the water it brought would not be enough to fill all the basins. When that happened the harvest was poor, and there was often famine. Occasionally the flood failed for several years in succession, and the famine was catastrophic. Records from the Nilometer at Roda show periods of several years when levels were high and others when they were low, but with no obvious pattern to the changes. When the flood was higher than normal it might breach the embankments, threatening to destroy the entire system.

That is why, around the middle of the 19th century, low dams were built to hold back the Nile waters, and canals to release small amounts every few weeks. This allowed farmers to grow two or three crops a year. Little by little, the Nile and its tributaries were brought under control. A bigger area of land could then be cultivated more dependably, and agricultural production increased.

There was still a need to extend the growing season by providing water throughout the year, and in the latter part of the 19th century six dams were constructed for this purpose, the last being at Aswân. It was completed in 1902 and heightened twice, in 1907 and between 1929 and 1934. Figure 11 shows its location, 3.5 miles (5.6 kilometers) upstream of the town. In its day it was one of the largest dams in the world, with a granite wall 1.5 miles (2.4 kilometers)

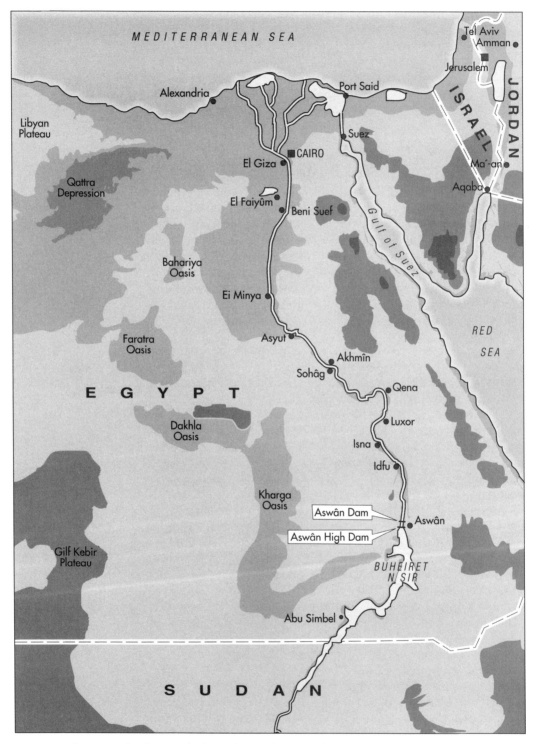

Figure 11: *Aswân Dams on the Nile River.*   (Dorling Kindersley Multimedia, 1995)

long that can fill a lake extending 150 miles (240 kilometers) upstream with more than 6,400 million cubic yards (4,893 million cubic meters) of water. There are 180 sluices in the wall. These allow most of the floodwater to pass almost unimpeded, taking its silt with it. Then, after the flood has peaked, the sluices are closed and water is stored for use during the dry season.

Dams can do more than just store water. A regular flow of water through or beside the wall can spin turbines and generate electricity. A generating plant fitted to the Aswân Dam began producing power in 1960.

That year work began on an even more ambitious project, the Aswân High Dam, 4 miles (6.4 kilometers) upstream of the original dam and built to a West German design subsequently modified by Soviet engineers. Its purpose was to free Egypt once and for all from its dependence on the annual Nile flood and, at the same time, to increase greatly the area of farmland and generate a substantial amount of electrical power. It took 8 years to build the dam wall and 2 more years to complete the installation of the 12 generating turbines. These were made in the Soviet Union, which sent 400 technicians to work on the project and also contributed one-third of the cost, of about $1 billion. At one time the construction employed about 33,000 workers.

On January 15, 1971, the dam was officially declared open. Its wall is 364 feet (109.2 meters) high, more than 3,000 feet (900 meters) thick at its base, and 2.3 miles (3.7 kilometers) long. It is difficult to imagine the size of the dam, but its volume is about 17 times that of the Great Pyramid at Giza. Its hydroelectric generators can produce 2.1 gigawatts of power (1 gigawatt = 1,000,000,000 watts; *gigawatt* is abbreviated "GW" and pronounced "jiggawatt"), enough to supply Egypt with 25 percent of its electricity.

Behind the dam lies its reservoir, Lake Nasser (labeled by its Arabic name, Buheiret Nâsir, in figure 11), named after Gamal Abdel Nasser, who was president of Egypt when the dam was built. It averages 6 miles (9.6 kilometers) in width and is 310 miles (496 kilometers) long, nearly one-third of it being across the border in Sudan.

From its inception, the dam project was controversial. All dams involve the flooding of low-lying land to form the reservoir. This is inevitable, but always unpopular, and the valley that was flooded to make Lake Nasser contained many ancient sites of great historic importance. An international project was launched in 1960, headed by the United Nations Educational, Scientific, and Cultural Organization (UNESCO), to save the 19 most important monuments. Several temples, including that at Abu Simbel, together with its huge statues, were removed entirely and reconstructed on high ground close to the new lake. The valley was also inhabited, of course, and all 100,000 people living there had to be evacuated and resettled.

Severe environmental problems were also predicted. Some materialized, but others did not, and they need to be set against the benefits the dam delivered. The aim was to supply enough irrigation water to increase the area of farmland by about 900,000 acres (360,000 hectares). This work started, but in 1979 a drought began and lasted for several years, lowering the water level in the lake by 20 percent. The water supply to farms had to be curtailed, and the power output was almost halved. Despite this setback, the output of corn and wheat increased steadily during the drought years, although rice production did not do so well.

The table shows the annual yield of these crops from 1971, the year the dam was completed, to 1994 (figures for 1987 and 1990 were not available). Yields are shown in two ways, as the amount produced (in thousands of metric tons; 1 tonne = 1.1 U.S. tons) and as indices. These are useful for comparing the output in different years. Yields for one base year—in this case, 1971—are given a value of 100, and yields for other years are calculated as percentages of the yield in the base year. In 1983, for example, the corn yield was 150 percent of the 1971 yield, the wheat yield 115 percent, and the rice yield 96 percent.

As the table shows, corn and wheat yields increased steadily, then leapt ahead around 1990. By then they had more than doubled since 1971. Rice yields lagged, often not reaching their 1971 level (index less than 100), but then they, too, began to increase around 1990; if the trend continues, they are likely to double the 1971 figures around the year 2000.

Whether yields continue to rise at these rates depends on major improvements in irrigation schemes. Egyptian farmers were used to cultivating basins, watered by the annual flood. Perennial irrigation calls for different techniques. When water is supplied to the surface, it drains quickly through the sandy soil. It is lost to the crops, but accumulates as groundwater, and slowly the water table rises. In some parts of Egypt it is rising at 6–10 feet (1.8–3 meters) per year and has already reached the root zone of plants. Effectively, the soil is becoming waterlogged and plant roots are deprived of air, which they need for respiration. Evaporation from the surface then draws water upward, but as it evaporates salts dissolved in it are deposited in the upper layer of soil. Most crop plants can tolerate only small concentrations of salts, and if those are exceeded, they die.

The remedy to both waterlogging and salt accumulation (called "salination") is to install efficient drainage. This removes surplus water. Unfortunately, it is expensive.

In the hot, dry climates of Egypt and Sudan, it was feared that much of the water in Lake Nasser would be lost by evaporation. This did not happen. A rich population of microscopic plants and

EGYPTIAN ANNUAL PRODUCTION OF THREE CEREAL CROPS
('000 metric tons; figures in parentheses are indices, 1971 = 100)

Year	Corn	Wheat	Rice
1971	2342 (100)	1729 (100)	2534 (100)
1972	2421 (103)	1618 (94)	2507 (99)
1973	2508 (107)	1838 (106)	2274 (90)
1974	2600 (111)	1850 (107)	2500 (99)
1975	2600 (111)	2033 (118)	2450 (97)
1976	2710 (115)	1960 (113)	2530 (100)
1977	2900 (124)	1872 (108)	2270 (90)
1978	3197 (136)	1933 (112)	2351 (93)
1979	2937 (125)	1856 (107)	2507 (99)
1980	3230 (138)	1796 (104)	2348 (93)
1981	3308 (141)	1806 (104)	2236 (88)
1982	2709 (116)	2016 (117)	2287 (90)
1983	3510 (150)	1996 (115)	2440 (96)
1984	3600 (154)	1815 (105)	2600 (103)
1985	3982 (170)	1874 (108)	2800 (110)
1986	3801 (162)	1929 (112)	2450 (97)
1987	Figures not available		
1988	4088 (174)	2839 (164)	1900 (75)
1989	3748 (160)	3148 (182)	2680 (106)
1990	Figures not available		
1991	5270 (225)	4483 (259)	3152 (124)
1992	5226 (223)	4618 (267)	3908 (154)
1993	5300 (226)	4786 (277)	3800 (150)
1994	4883 (208)	4437 (257)	4582 (181)

animals established itself in the warm water, rich in nutrients carried by the river. Fish were introduced, or arrived by themselves, to feed there, and Lake Nasser now supports a thriving fishing industry.

In addition to water, the dam traps and holds the silt carried by the Nile. This settles to the bed of the lake. Eventually it will raise the bed so much that the dam will be useless, but it will be several centuries before that happens. This is partly because much of the silt is collecting at the southern end of the lake. One day this will reach the surface and dry, providing a small area of land for the use of the Sudanese.

Downstream, of course, the fields no longer receive their annual load of nutritious sediment. Farmers have to compensate for the loss of nutrients by using factory-made fertilizer.

Now that water flows at much the same rate throughout the year, the Nile itself has changed. Its water has become more salty, because of salts entering from adjacent fields, and it is contaminated by fertilizer and pesticides. This has reduced the number and variety of fish, partly offsetting the benefits of the Lake Nasser fishery, and it has also reduced the quality of water people use for washing and drinking. The lack of silt has led to erosion along the banks of the river and in the delta, where the coast is receding and salt water is infiltrating into the groundwater (see page 75). Silt no longer reaches the Mediterranean, where it used to nourish organisms supporting an important sardine fishery. Sardine fishing in the eastern Mediterranean has almost disappeared.

Finally, the presence of water throughout the year has led to an increase in diseases transmitted by aquatic organisms. Schistosomiasis (or bilharzia) is probably the most widespread of these. It is not fatal, but its victims become weak and apathetic and it can lead to more serious secondary infections. It can be treated with drugs, but victims are easily reinfected.

Schistosomiasis is caused by a microscopic animal called a fluke, or trematode, belonging to the genus *Schistosoma* (there are 3 species). Fluke eggs hatch in water, and the larvae enter the body of an aquatic snail. There they develop into small, fork-tailed animals (called cercariae) that leave the snail and swim around in the water until they find a mammal, which may be a human. They discard their tails and burrow through the skin, feeding on glycogen in the blood, and are carried to the lungs and then to the heart and liver, growing all the time. When mature, they mate and lay eggs that leave the body in urine or feces, and the cycle begins again. Before the dam was built, many of the snails died during the dry season; this restricted the numbers of *Schistosoma* flukes. Now more of the snails can survive, and the flukes are spreading. Schistosomiasis has become a serious problem in the Nile delta, and it is spreading south along the Nile valley.

Overall, the benefits of the Aswân High Dam greatly outweigh the harm it has done. Nevertheless, experience shows that interfering with the natural behavior of a river has consequences reaching far beyond those associated with the management of its water flow.

Wet Rice Farming

Floods usually cause huge amounts of damage to property, destroy crops, and kill people, but some floods are encouraged. Where flooding can be relied on and controlled, it can be used, and Asian farmers have been using it for thousands of years. Whenever you eat rice in any form, including rice-based breakfast cereals and snacks, almost certainly floods helped in its production. Oil obtained from rice bran is used in making some margarine, so even that food may have been produced with at least some assistance from floods. In southern and eastern Asia, where rice is the central part of the diet, the floods bring life, not death.

Rice is the second most important food in the world, after wheat. Each year, farmers throughout the world grow more than 500 million tons (550 million tonnes) of it (measured as the edible grain, after it has been milled to remove the husks), compared with about 600 million tons (660 million tonnes) of wheat. Most is eaten in the region where it was grown, and almost all of it is grown in Asia. Of all the wheat grown in the world, about 20 percent is exported, but only about 5 percent of rice is exported. Much of the exported rice is grown in the United States.

China alone produces about 206 million tons (226.6 million tonnes) a year, more than 40 percent of the world total. Together China, India (122 million tons, or 134.2 million tonnes), Indonesia (51 million tons, or 56.1 million tonnes), Vietnam (25 million tons, or 27.5 million tonnes), Thailand (20 million tons, or 22 million tonnes), Japan (16.5 million tons, or 18.6 million tonnes), and North and South Korea (10 million tons, or 11 million tonnes) grow 90 percent of all the rice in the world; the output from smaller Asian producers brings the Asian total to about 95 percent of total world production.

Figure 12: *Workers plant rice cuttings in a flooded field at the Central Rice Research Institute in Cuttack, India.* (United Nations)

No one knows where rice was first cultivated, but the modern plant is most probably descended from a plant that once grew wild over much of southern Asia. A different species, native to West Africa, was domesticated there. By 2800 B.C. rice was a regular part of the diet in China. The Chinese may have learned of it from India —certainly, Indians were eating it at about that time—although it may have been grown even earlier in Thailand. Rice chaff has been found at Non Nok Tha, an archaeological site in northeast Thailand dated at 4500–4000 B.C., and traces of it have been found in China and dated to around 5000 B.C., but neither of these necessarily came from cultivated rice.

Knowledge of rice cultivation spread to the Middle East, and the invading Saracens brought it to Europe in the Middle Ages. Rice is still grown in southern Europe and used in traditional dishes such as paella and risotto. It was first grown in North America in 1685, in South Carolina, and spread to North Carolina and Georgia by the early 19th century; its cultivation moved westward after the Civil War, to Louisiana, Texas, Arkansas, and eventually to California, where it is now one of the 10 most economically important farm crops.

Today rice is grown in many parts of the world, in latitudes as high as 53° (the latitude of Edmonton, Alberta) and in mountains up to 8,000 feet (2,400 meters); however, about 80 percent of all rice is grown in the lowlands in low latitudes. It thrives best, and produces the biggest yields, in fields that are flooded for part of the year.

Rice is a grass, related to the other cultivated cereals, but different from them in one respect. Like most plants, cereal grasses cannot tolerate waterlogged soil. Their roots need air for respiration, and in water they drown. The roots of rice plants also need air, but rice stems are hollow, and provided the upper part of the plant stands clear of the water surface, air reaches the roots through the stem. Rice can be grown on dry land, when it is known as "upland rice"; that is how it has to be grown in the hills (hence the name), beyond the reach of flood waters. Less than one-fifth of the world crop is grown this way, however, because upland rice produces much lower yields than "wet" rice, although the rice itself is no different.

There are two cultivated species, *Oryza sativa* and *Oryza glaberrima*. The West African species, *O. glaberrima*, is known as "red rice" from the color of its bran; it is rarely grown elsewhere. American wild rice, also known as Indian rice and Tuscarora rice (*Zizania aquatica*) is also a grass, native to eastern North America. It resembles the rice plant, but is not closely related to *Oryza*.

The rice we eat, and the one eaten in Asia, is *O. sativa*, of which there are two types, or subspecies, *indica* and *japonica*, with tens of thousands of varieties of each main type. *Indica* rice has long grains that are separate after cooking. *Japonica* grains are round and stick together when they are cooked. Cooked and dried *japonica* grains are used to make rice flakes, rice crispies, and puffed rice.

After harvesting, the rice sheaves are stacked and left to dry for a few days, then the grain is separated by threshing and winnowing to remove the chaff. The grain is milled to remove the husk. It is then brown rice, which many people prefer. Brown rice retains the layer below the husk, called the bran (the aleurone layer, rich in enzymes and thiamin), and the germ (from which a new plant will grow). A second milling removes these, and the grains are passed through brushes to remove any remaining particles of bran or husk. In some countries the rice is then polished, by coating it with talc and glucose.

About one-fifth of the world rice harvest is parboiled before its first milling, a technique most popular in India and southern Asia. Parboiling involves soaking the rice, with its husks, for one or two days, then heating it for a short time in a sealed vessel with very little water, and allowing it to dry before milling. This alters the outer layer of the starchy endosperm, toughening the grains so fewer break during milling; although parboiled rice takes a little longer to cook, its grains do not stick together. It is also more nutritious than rice that has not been parboiled, because the part of the endosperm affected by parboiling absorbs thiamin (vitamin B1) from the bran, thus reducing the amount lost during cooking.

When rice is grown on dry land, the technique is the same as that for growing wheat. The land is plowed and harrowed and the seeds sown in rows. For wet rice, the technique is different.

Many American rice growers drop seed and fertilizer together from airplanes into flooded fields, and spray pesticide later, also from the air. Together with machines for harvesting, this has reduced the number of person-hours per acre from 900 to about 7; traditionally, however—and until recently in America, too—growing rice has been hard, back-breaking work.

The seeds, comprising rice grains with their husks, are soaked in water for 24 hours, then stored for a day or two until they start to germinate. At that stage they are sown in dry soil, where they grow for a month.

Meanwhile, the other land is prepared. The fields are low-lying and surrounded by banks, called "bunds," and after the surface has been tilled, it must be level. Water is then allowed to flood the fields. Most are flooded to a depth of about 4 inches (10.2 centimeters), but for some varieties the rice is planted in dry ground that is then flooded, and the water is deeper. Once the field has been flooded it is called a "paddy"; the name "paddy" is also given to the rice itself just after it has been harvested. Transplanting the seedlings from the nursery into the paddies, about 6 inches (15.24 centimeters) apart in rows about 12 inches (30.5 centimeters) apart, is sometimes done by machines, but often by hand, by women and children who must spend long hours bent almost double with their feet and hands in water.

As the crop starts to ripen, the water is drained from the field and the ground dries. With modern varieties, the crop is ready to harvest after about 17 weeks. Traditional varieties ripen more slowly, and the introduction of new varieties as part of the "Green Revolution" has meant two crops a year can often be grown where only one grew before. In some places annual yields have increased eightfold.

Water is the key to the entire operation, and the best rice-growing land is on the floodplains and deltas of large rivers. Rice is grown in the deltas of the Red River and Mekong in Vietnam, the Chao Phraya in Thailand, and the Brahmaputra and Ganges in India and Bangladesh.

Southern Asia is affected by the monsoons. During the winter monsoon, the climate is dry, but the summer monsoon brings heavy rain to swell the rivers. These tend to overflow their banks anyway, often with disastrous consequences, but it is this natural flood of which the rice farmers take advantage, allowing the water to inundate the paddies and drain from them when the rains have eased and the river levels have fallen. Elsewhere, the fields must be flooded artificially, by means of irrigation canals, and outside the monsoon regions many ingenious irrigation systems have been devised over the thousands of years people have been growing rice.

Despite the fact that rice grows under conditions that would destroy any other cereal crop, rice farmers are as dependent as any others on the weather. The floods are needed, but only at certain times and to certain depths. Monsoon rains are not always reliable. In some years they arrive late, or fail to arrive at all, and in others they are so heavy they wash over the paddies and carry away the crops. Outside the monsoon region, drought destroys rice more quickly than it can destroy wheat, and heavy rain or hail shortly before harvest can wreak just as much damage to rice as to wheat.

Where floods happen

Bourke, in New South Wales, Australia, receives a little more than 13 inches (33 centimeters) of rain in most years. The climate is dry, and Bourke is more than 400 miles (640 kilometers) from the sea. People in Alice Springs, in the Northern Territory, expect about 10 inches (25.4 centimeters) of rain a year. Over much of Australia, water is a valuable resource, used with care. In the summer of 1973–74, however, the weather was different. It rained heavily and persistently. Rivers rose and overflowed their banks. Thousands of sheep drowned, and floodwaters covered large areas of New South Wales, Queensland, and the vast desert of the interior. Nothing like it had ever been known, although there have been extensive floods in southeastern Australia. In 1955, 40,000 people from 40 New South Wales towns were made homeless when the Macquarie, Castlereagh, Namoi, Hunter, and Gwydir rivers overflowed, and in 1956 floods inundated an area 40 miles (64 kilometers) wide, also in New South Wales, between the towns of Hay and Balranald, both on the Murrumbidgee River.

Ulan Bator, capital of Mongolia, is 4,347 feet (1,304 meters) above sea level, and about as far from the sea as it is possible to be. It also has a dry climate, with an average of only about 8.2 inches (20.9 centimeters) of rain a year, making it drier even than Alice Springs. Yet it was flooded in August 1996, when two rivers overflowed.

The 1973–74 Australian and 1996 Mongolian floods were very rare events, however. If a desert can be flooded, clearly floods can

Figure 13: *Floodwaters of the Feather River rush through a break in the levee at Nicolaus, Sutter County, California, on December 24, 1955.* (U.S. Geological Survey/W. L. Hofmann)

happen anywhere, but these were the kind of floods that might be expected only once in several centuries.

Hydrologists, the scientists who study the movement of water, rate the severity of floods by the probability of their occurrence. Before the Aswân High Dam was built, the Nile overflowed its banks every year, inundating land to either side throughout much of Egypt (see page 31). Hydrologists would rate the Nile flood as a "one-year flood," meaning the amount of flooding people should expect to happen once a year. Similarly, high tides (see page 65) flood beaches regularly and are not really counted as floods, but every so often an especially high tide, driven by onshore winds, may carry water higher up the shore. If this happens fairly often it may count as a one-year flood. If it happens less often, it may be a 10-year or 100-year flood. As figure 14 illustrates, a one-year coastal flood may carry water some distance into the shore vegetation, which comprises wetland plants that are not harmed by the water. A 100-year flood carries it much higher, into vegetation that is not adapted to inundation by sea water.

A flood that happens, on average, once a year causes little harm. Plants can cope with it, and if it affects a town or village, defenses can be built against it. Even the scale of flooding that is likely to happen only once in a century is frequent enough to warrant measures to protect property. The assessment is purely statistical and not a prediction. Scientists study past records and then calculate the probability of a flood extending to a particular area in any one

Figure 14: *Shoreland zones likely to flood.*

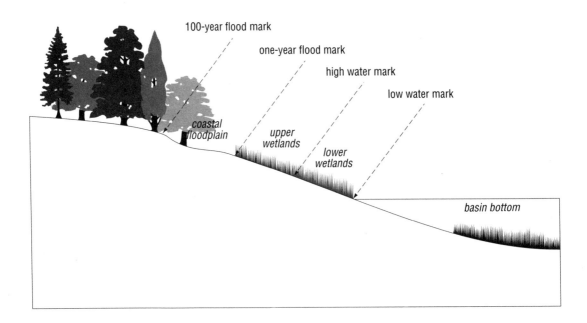

year as one chance in so many. If they estimate there is a 1-in-10 chance, it is called a "10-year flood." This does not mean floods of this scale will occur at 10-year intervals. The Mississippi overflowed to produce a 10-year flood in 1943 and then again in 1944, 1947, and 1953.

There are other floods, however, that are expected to occur much less frequently than this. It is difficult, perhaps impossible, to provide adequate protection against an event that can be expected only once in a thousand years, or even less frequently than that. The flood that devastated the small English village of Lynmouth in 1952 (see page 48) was rated a 50,000-year flood. This is not to say that a similar flood occurred there 50,000 years ago (during the last ice age!), but only that the 1952 flood was an exceedingly rare event. It is these very rare floods that cause most damage, because they are so unexpected.

Although it may be rare, low-lying coastal regions are almost bound to be flooded by the sea occasionally unless sea walls are built to keep out the water. Unfortunately, coastal areas are popular places to live, so large numbers of people live under this threat. Land along most of the Atlantic coast of the United States lies close to sea level. Miami is only 25 feet (7.5 meters) above sea level; Norfolk, Virginia, 11 feet (3.3 meters); and Charleston, South Carolina, only 9 feet (2.7 meters). Along much of the Atlantic coastal plain, shown in figure 15, the coastline itself is sandy. People enjoy walking and playing on sandy beaches and, naturally enough, these are favorite places to build homes. This is unwise, because sandy coasts are also the most vulnerable. Sand is often unstable. Dunes move, slowly but perceptibly, and the sand barrier standing between homes and the shore may vanish. Some years ago, at Bude, a resort with a popular sandy beach in southwest England, a storm lowered the beach by 6 feet (1.8 meters) in a single night.

To add to the risk, the Atlantic and Gulf coasts lie on the track of hurricanes. These develop over the tropical Atlantic, cross the Caribbean, then swing northward as they approach the American coast. Whether they cross the coast is a matter of chance, but many do and those which miss, remaining out at sea, may still generate large waves that can cause storm surges (see page 64) capable of causing flooding for a considerable distance inland.

Low-lying coastal plains are not confined to North America, of course. They are found on all continents, and such areas are always prone to flooding, even in latitudes too high to experience hurricanes. In northwest Europe, for example, there are extensive coastal areas lying very close to sea level. The northern part of Flanders, in Belgium, is almost at sea level. In the Netherlands, 2,500 square miles (6,500 square kilometers), amounting to 19 percent of the total land area, is land reclaimed from the sea forming level fields,

coastal plain

called "polders," protected by dikes that must be maintained constantly.

Away from coasts, the level land along the floodplain of a large river is also likely to flood, not by the migration of the meander system (see page 19), but because heavy rain or melting snow far upstream loads the river with more water than its banks can hold. The Mississippi, meandering south toward the Gulf, has overflowed many times. Rains that began in August 1926 caused it and its tributaries to inundate more than 25,000 square miles (65,000 square kilometers) in seven states. In places the floods were 80 miles (128 kilometers) across and 18 feet (5.4 meters) deep, and they did not recede until July of the following year. In January 1937 the river flooded again, destroying 13,000 homes, and at the end of April 1973 it inundated nearly 1,000 square miles (2,600 square kilometers). In the summer of 1993, the overflowing Mississippi caused damage costing $12 billion in nine states.

The Mississippi is not unique, of course, and its floods are not the worst in the world. Several Asian rivers must share that notoriety. One is the Yellow River (Huang Ho) in China. Its flood of 1887 inundated at least 1,500 towns and villages. Estimates of the number of people it killed range from 900,000 to 2.5 million. In 1931 another of its floods left 80 million people homeless.

The other great Chinese river, the Yangtze, flowing 3,400 miles (5,440 kilometers) from the Himalayas to the East China Sea, also floods. Ordinarily, it discharges less than six million U.S. gallons (22.8 liters) of water each second, but at times this can double, causing the river to inundate a plain to either side covering 70,000 square miles (182,000 square kilometers). This plain is home to some 250 million people, and the land there is fertile, producing a substantial proportion of the nation's grain crop. In 1931, the same year that the Yellow River overflowed, heavy rain caused the Yangtze to rise 97 feet (29.1 meters) above its normal level. The resulting flood destroyed crops, leading to famine and disease and a death toll of more than 3.7 million people. In the summer of 1996, the Yangtze, its tributaries, and other rivers farther south caused widespread flooding in which more than 2,000 people died.

Some Asian countries suffer flooding from both rivers and the sea. Vietnam, for example, has two large, fertile river deltas. In the north, the Red River (Song Hong) flows into the Gulf of Tonkin, and in the south the Mekong flows into the South China Sea. The climate is affected by the summer monsoon. Da Nang, only 10 feet (3 meters) above sea level, receives almost 38 inches (96.5 centimeters) of rain in September and October. Both deltas lie close to the tracks of typhoons (hurricanes that occur in the western Pacific and China Sea). In July and August 1996, the country suffered a succession of tropical storms, verging on typhoons. Hanoi was flooded when the Red River burst its banks.

Korea also suffers, but Bangladesh is the country most severely affected. All but about 10 percent of the country lies in the deltas of the Ganges and Brahmaputra rivers (known there as the Padma and Jamuna). These discharge into the Bay of Bengal, a sea area where cyclones (the local name for hurricanes) form and move north. When the monsoon rains swell the two rivers, they merge, so floods are commonplace; many homes are built on stilts to keep them clear of the water. Despite this, every year people die in floods and storms, even when the rains are no heavier than normal. If the monsoon is heavier than usual, or a cyclone causes a storm surge, the stilts are not enough protection, and the resulting disaster is often severe, because the country is very densely populated. The total population is about 120 million, and the average population density more than 2,000 people per square mile. The 1996 monsoon was heavy, and flooding began in early July. Both the Padma and Jamuna overflowed; at least half a million people were forced to leave their homes, and more than 120 died.

Low-lying coastal plains and level river valleys are where floods are most likely. Where both occur in the same place, as they do along the deltas of major rivers, it is inevitable that land will be flooded from time to time.

Flash floods

Lynmouth and Lynton are twin coastal villages in Devon, in southwest England—Lynton to the west and Lynmouth to the east of Lyn Mouth, where the river Lyn meets the sea. The Lyn is a single river for only a very short distance. Just inland of the villages it is formed by the meeting of two smaller rivers, the East Lyn and West Lyn. Between them, these drain about 38 square miles (98.8 square kilometers) of Exmoor, an upland moor. Exmoor is fairly high, and on its northern side forms a plateau, called the Chains. From there, the two Lyns fall through narrow, wooded valleys 1,500 feet (450 meters) in 4 miles (6.4 kilometers) before joining, then plunge farther from that point to the sea. The villages attract many tourists, drawn by the villages themselves, the sandy beach, the moorland, and the beauty of the steep valleys.

In the first two weeks of August 1952, however, the vacationers were not having a good time. The weather was miserable. The rain was not constant, but it was often heavy. It thoroughly soaked the ground up on the moor. On Friday, August 15, the rain was persistent and the sky so dark that the lights were on in many of the houses. That evening the rain intensified. In the course of 24 hours, 9.11 inches (23.13 centimeters) of rain were recorded at one place and 7.58 inches (19.25 centimeters) at another. Most of it fell between 8:00 P.M. and 1:00 A.M. on the 16th. It was later estimated that, by then, three billion tons of rain had fallen onto the area drained by the two rivers. At 7:30 P.M. the hydroelectric plant supplying power to the area was overwhelmed when the canal feeding water to it turned into a raging torrent, and at 9:00 P.M. the diesel emergency system also failed. Lynmouth and Lynton were in darkness; the two rivers were carrying so much water that at times they formed waves 30 feet (9 meters) high. Up to 23,000 cubic feet, or 621 cubic meters (575 tons, or 632.5 tonnes) of water per second fell down a very steep incline, dislodging huge boulders and then rolling them forward. In all, around 200,000 cubic yards (152,911 cubic meters) of boulders, soil, and other debris were washed downstream.

For a time, the valley of the West Lyn was blocked by fallen trees; water pressure finally burst through this temporary dam, however. That is when most of the damage occurred, as surging water destroyed stone bridges and demolished houses.

The following morning, boulders weighing up to 15 tons (16.5 tonnes) each covered the beach; about 40,000 tons (44,000 tonnes) of them were piled up in Lynmouth itself. Altogether, 93 houses had been damaged beyond repair or swept out to sea,

132 cars had been washed into the sea, and debris littered the beaches for miles on either side of Lyn Mouth. The flash flood killed 34 people.

This was rated a 50,000-year flood (see page 45), although the Lyn had never been known to behave that way before, so there is no previous flood with which to compare it. Nor has it flooded since. Lynmouth has now been rebuilt and is once more an attractive and popular resort.

Flash floods always happen suddenly; it is the element of surprise, combined with the violence they can sometimes inflict, that makes them so dangerous. It is easy to understand why they happen, but very difficult to predict them.

In the case of the Lynmouth flash flood, prolonged rain over the drainage basin of the two rivers had delivered water faster than it could be removed. The water table had risen, and the land was thoroughly sodden. The rivers were flowing strongly, their levels high, but they showed no indication of being about to overflow their banks. Then a single rainstorm tipped the balance. The mechanism was simple. What was difficult was predicting the storm that triggered the flood. It was very localized and lasted for only a few hours. Had the rain occurred only a mile or two away, it would have fallen over the sea or over a larger drainage basin, and there would have been no flash flood.

The land does not need to be soaked in order for flash floods to occur. Flooding can also happen when the ground is very dry. Then it is the intensity of the rainfall that causes the flooding. Water falls to the ground much faster than it can soak into the soil, and so it flows directly into previously dry gullies, turning them into fast-flowing, turbulent rivers channeling vast amounts of water onto the low-lying ground where people are most likely to have their homes. This is what happened on September 2, 1996, around the town of al-Geili, in Sudan. Two hours of heavy rain caused flash floods that destroyed rail lines, bridges, and many houses. The flood left 15 people dead and thousands homeless.

Whether the ground is wet or dry, it is a big storm that brings enough rain in a sufficiently short time to cause the flooding. Rain of this intensity is often called a "cloudburst." This is not a term meteorologists use, but it is fairly descriptive of what happens. Before the storm arrives, the air is warm and moist (in Lynmouth it was summer and had been raining, although it is the air that should be moist, not necessarily the ground). If the sky is clear at first, gradually a high-level cloud covers it. This is the "anvil" at the top of the storm cloud, extending a long way in front of it. More usually, the sky is already cloudy or hazy and just becomes a little darker. Any wind that has been blowing may cease, because air is now being drawn into the base of the storm cloud, canceling out the wind. This is the "calm before the storm." Then it grows much

Latent heat and dewpoint

Water can exist in three different states, or phases: gas (water vapor), liquid (water), and solid (ice). In the gaseous phase, molecules are free to move in all directions. In the liquid phase, molecules join together in short "strings." In the solid phase, molecules form a closed structure with a space at the center.

Molecules bond to one another by the attraction of opposite charges, and energy must be supplied to break those bonds. This energy is absorbed by the molecules without changing their temperature, and the same amount of energy is released when the bonds form again. This is called "latent heat." For pure water, 600 calories of energy are absorbed to change 1 gram (1 g = 0.035 oz) from liquid to gas (evaporation) and 80 calories to melt 1 gram of ice. Sublimation, the direct change from ice to vapor without passing through the liquid phase, absorbs 680 calories for each gram (the sum of the latent heats of melting and evaporation). In each case, the same amount of energy is released when water vapor condenses into liquid water and when water freezes.

Energy to supply the latent heat is taken from the surrounding air or water. When ice melts or water evaporates, the air and water in contact with them are cooled, because energy has been taken from them.

When latent heat is released by freezing and condensation, the surroundings are warmed. This is very important in the formation of storm clouds. It warms the air further, making it rise higher.

The amount of water vapor air can hold depends on its temperature: Warm air can hold more water vapor than cool air. If moist air is cooled, its water vapor will condense into liquid droplets. The temperature at which this occurs is called the "dewpoint." It is the temperature at which dew forms on surfaces and evaporates from them. When moist air rises and cools, the height at which it cools to its dewpoint temperature is called the "condensation level"; it marks the base of clouds.

darker. This is because the cloud now overhead is densely packed with water droplets and reaches a height of 35,000 feet (10,500 meters) or more, blocking out the sunlight. Then the wind starts again and the sky lightens (although in Lynmouth it was evening by this point). Overhead, the cloud now consists mainly of water drops, much bigger than cloud droplets and less opaque, falling in the downdraft of air from the cloud that produces the wind. With a cloud of this size, there is often lightning and thunder as well.

Inside the cloud, warm air is rising, drawing in more air from below the cloud base. As it rises, the air expands and cools. The cloud base is the height at which the air is cool enough for water vapor to start condensing into liquid droplets. Condensation releases latent heat (see box above), warming the surrounding air and making it rise more. This cools it again, causing more condensation and more warming of the surrounding air, and the air rises still farther.

Eventually the air rises to a height beyond which it can rise no further, because it is at the same density as the air above it. This marks the cloud top. In a storm cloud, where the rising air currents are very vigorous, the top of the cloud is so high that water vapor sublimes directly into ice, forming tiny crystals. High-level winds then sweep these from the top of the cloud, forming the anvil shape often seen at the top of the large cumulonimbus storm clouds.

The crystals fall slowly. When they reach a level where the air is warmer, they melt. Melting absorbs latent heat, cooling the air, and makes the air sink farther, and friction between the droplets and air drags cold air downward. The cloud then contains both

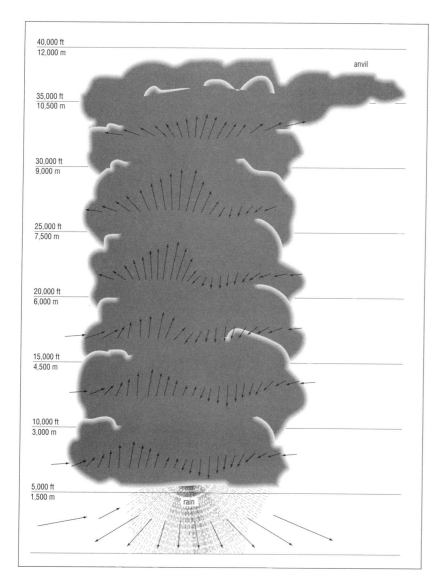

Figure 16: *Air currents in a storm cloud.*

40,000 ft
12,000 m

anvil

35,000 ft
10,500 m

30,000 ft
9,000 m

25,000 ft
7,500 m

20,000 ft
6,000 m

15,000 ft
4,500 m

10,000 ft
3,000 m

5,000 ft
1,500 m

rain

updrafts and downdrafts, as shown in figure 16. Falling water droplets collide and merge with one another, like the drops that trickle down a windowpane. They grow larger, but only the heaviest of them continue falling all the way through the cloud and out of the base, as rain. The others are picked up again by updrafts and swept to a higher level, from where they start their descent once more.

Eventually, however, the updrafts and downdrafts conflict. The downdrafts suppress the updrafts. This robs the cloud of the mechanism by which it grows and sustains itself. Usually, the rain will continue for a time as the cloud dissipates and vanishes. A cumulonimbus cloud rarely survives for more than an hour or so, but if the conditions that produced it continue, another will form to take its place.

With some clouds, the end is more dramatic, but it all happens so quickly that identifying the individual short-lived cloud which will die violently is impossible. In this case, the updrafts cease—there are only downdrafts, and the cloud collapses, releasing all its water droplets. This is what produces a cloudburst, and if the cloud was very large, the rain may continue for some time. There is a lot of water to release. A fully developed, large cumulonimbus cloud may contain 250,000 tons (275,000 tonnes) of water or more. If all of that falls over an area of 10 square miles (26 square kilometers), it will amount to almost 40 tons (44 tonnes) per acre, which is equivalent to 4 inches (10.16 centimeters) of rain; as one cloud collapses, another is likely to be forming, so the rain continues.

That much water rushing down a steep hillside will dislodge rocks and soil. It is not only the water people fear, but the landslides and mudslides. In two days in July 1996, 20 inches (50.8 centimeters) of rain fell along the border between North and South Korea. The South Koreans have built military barracks into the steep hillsides along the border. A mudslide buried more than 20 soldiers in one of these barracks, and landslides and mudslides engulfed three other units, one an air force base, and several guard posts. In North Korea, the floods destroyed much of the rice crop.

A week later at Biescas on the Spanish side of the Pyrenees, the mountain range between France and Spain, more than 70 vacationers died in a flash flood at a crowded campsite and trailer park. Light rain that suddenly turned into a torrential cloudburst sent floodwater, rocks, and mud through the Virgen de las Nieves site. Cars, tents, campers, and trailers were carried away in the swiftly flowing rivers of mud and rock, and trees were torn from the ground and scattered. Rescuers said the scene when they arrived was like a battlefield.

At the same time as the Biescas flash flood, Jhagraku, a remote village about 55 miles (88 kilometers) northeast of Katmandu, Nepal, was also being devastated in the same way. The rains triggered landslides that carried away dozens of homes and killed at least 40 people.

Such events are common, and there was nothing unusual about the summer of 1996. In addition to the floods in Korea, Spain, and Nepal, between June and August there were flash floods and landslides around Lake Maggiore, Italy; a mudslide buried a house at La Baie, Québec; and flash floods caused widespread damage on either side of the Saguenay River 200 miles (320 kilometers) north of Montréal. At Buffalo Creek, Colorado, the South Platte River overflowed suddenly, destroying a bridge and two roads. Near the Italian ski resort of Cortina d'Ampezzo, landslides and mudslides filled homes with rocks and mud, and in southeast England a flash flood left parts of Folkestone, Kent, under 6 feet (1.8 meters) of water.

When flash floods sweep through towns, they always cause a huge amount of damage, but sometimes there is one even more devastating than most. The Lynmouth tragedy in England has many parallels. In August 1955, Putnam, Connecticut, suffered a similar disaster. A manufacturing town, with a population then of more than 8,000, Putnam lies on the Quinebaug River, which divides the town into two parts and is crossed by three bridges. Rainstorms delivered 4 inches (10.16 centimeters) of rain, and a week later the dying remains of a hurricane added a further 8 inches (12.8 centimeters) in 24 hours. Upstream of Putnam there was a series of old dams. The increased water flow built up behind the first, broke through it, and carried debris from it to the second. One by one the dams collapsed, releasing a wall of water moving at up to 25 MPH (40 KPH) and throwing waves several feet high over the riverbanks. As it swept through the town, the river carried away all three bridges, roads including the main street, and railroad tracks, and damaged about one-quarter of all the buildings. It also caused huge explosions when it washed through a warehouse stocked with barrels of magnesium; the magnesium exploded on contact with the water, and the river carried blazing barrels downstream. It was a week before the flood subsided and the extent of the damage could be assessed. The cost was estimated at $13 million, but no lives were lost. The emergency services had acted swiftly to evacuate people as soon as there was a risk of the dams failing.

When large rivers in the lowlands overflow, they do so gently; the rising waters give warning. It is small rivers, carrying water a short distance down steep slopes, that are most likely to be overwhelmed by a sudden increase in the volume of water flowing into them and cause devastating flash floods.

Tsunamis

Soon after 10:00 A.M. August 27, 1883, a wall of water 120 feet (36 meters) high, racing across the sea, struck the coasts of Java and Sumatra, in what is now Indonesia. Towns and villages in its path were demolished, and about 36,000 people died. Similar waves, though too small to cause harm, were recorded in Hawaii and South America, thousands of miles away.

It was the kind of wave people dread most. Waves of this type are much bigger than ordinary sea waves, although rarely as high as the 1883 one, and they arrive without obvious warning, traveling very fast. People used to call them "tidal waves," but they have nothing to do with the tide. Others called them simply "great sea waves," but out at sea they are so small sailors are unaware of them as they pass. The Japanese call them *tsunamis*, or "harbor waves." This is a much more accurate name, and the one now generally used.

They are not common, but every year there are a few. In 1996 one killed 12 people in Peru. About 60 people were killed by one in northern Honshu, Japan, on May 26, 1983, and another struck the coast of Nicaragua on September 1, 1992, killing 105 people and injuring 489. Indonesia suffered one on June 3, 1994. It struck during the night, killing more than 200 people while they slept. Nor are tsunamis confined to coasts facing the Pacific, although that is where most occur. Two tsunamis, up to 10 feet (3 meters) high, struck a 60-mile (96-kilometer) stretch of the French Mediterranean coast on October 16, 1979. Eleven people were swept away in Nice and one in Antibes, and were presumed dead.

Tsunamis are often destructive, sometimes extremely so. At Sanriku, Japan, a tsunami killed about 25,000 people in 1896 and then went on to cause severe damage in California, Chile, and Hawaii. The largest in this century happened in April 1946, in Hawaii. It destroyed the waterfront in the city of Hilo, killing 96 people. Not all are big and dangerous, however. One tsunami recorded at Hachijo Island, Japan, on September 5, 1996, was only 10 inches (25.4 centimeters) high, and still smaller ones were registered on other offshore islands. A 10-inch wave will harm no one. If you were on the beach when it arrived, you might not even notice it. Nevertheless, it was a tsunami, small or not.

They are not tidal, but tsunamis are certainly waves and obey the laws governing the behavior of waves. There are several kinds of waves. Fasten one end of a long rope to a support, hold the other end, and move it up and down; a series of waves will travel along the rope. They will look much like the wave shown in

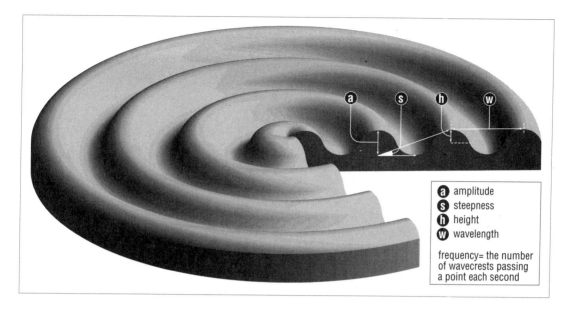

a amplitude
s steepness
h height
w wavelength

frequency= the number
of wavecrests passing
a point each second

figure 17. The waves travel, but obviously the rope itself moves only up and down. It does not jump from your hand and gather itself in a tangle against the support. Sea waves also travel but, like the rope, the water itself moves only up and down, not forward. If it did, all the sea would pile up on land. Throw a stone into the still water of a pond, and waves will move outward from the disturbance as a series of circles, but the water does not actually accumulate at the edges of the pond. Leaves floating on the surface will bob up and down as each wave passes, but they will not travel with the forward moving energy of the wave, as surfers do.

What moves is not the water or the rope, but the energy that set it in motion, and the amount of energy imparted to the water can be calculated from the characteristics of the waves produced. The amplitude of a wave is the vertical distance from the lowest point in each trough to the highest point on each crest. The height of the wave is the vertical distance from the midpoint to the crest of each wave. As the name suggests, it is the height the wave reaches above the average level of the surface, and therefore it is equal to half the amplitude. The distance between one wavecrest and the next is the wavelength.

As small children soon learn in the bathtub, big disturbances make big waves. At sea, waves are produced by the wind; the stronger the wind, the bigger the waves it will make. A wind blowing steadily over a long enough stretch of water (called the "fetch") will raise waves proportional to the wind force. A moderate breeze, for example, blowing at about 20 MPH (32 KPH), will produce waves about 5 feet (1.5 meters) high; a fresh gale, blowing at about 40 MPH (64 KPH), will raise waves about 25 feet (7.5

Figure 17: *Properties of waves.*

meters) high; and a wind of 75 MPH (120 KPH), just strong enough to count as hurricane force, will generate waves 50 feet (15 meters) high. Real hurricanes can drive waves to even greater heights (see page 64).

Bathtubs may be too small to demonstrate the fact, but the size of the disturbance may also affect the speed with which waves travel. This is measured as the frequency or period. The frequency is the number of wavecrests that pass a fixed point in a certain time, usually one second, and the period is the time that elapses between one crest passing and the next. Finally, the steepness of the wave is important. This is calculated by dividing the height by the wavelength, but in fact it is the angle to the horizontal made by a line drawn from the trough of one wave to the crest of the next.

If you watch closely when you throw a stone into a pond, you will see that not all the waves are the same. Some have a longer period than others, and if the pond is big enough you will see that the slow-moving, long-period waves travel ahead of faster, short-period waves. The short-period waves move from the site of the disturbance, overtaking the waves ahead of them until they reach the front, but as they do so their period increases and they slow down. The group of waves as a whole travels at half the speed of the individual short-period waves, and at sea, waves always travel as groups. Over the open sea, eventually only the long-period waves remain as ocean swell, which can travel very long distances. Storms in Antarctic waters have been detected as swell as far away as Alaska.

There is something else you may notice in the pond. Floating leaves rise and fall as each wave passes, but they also move forward just a little way with the crest and back again with the trough. This is because the water itself is moving in small circles, forward with the crest and backward with the trough. You can think of this circular motion, shown in figure 18, as the movement of small "particles" of water. At the surface, the size of the circles they describe is related to the height of the waves. Beneath the surface the size of the circles decreases with depth until they disappear entirely at a depth equal to half the wavelength.

Waves are caused by disturbance. That disturbance transfers energy to the water, and the energy moves away from the source, passing from one set of water "particles" to the next. For most waves, the wind is the original source of energy, but not for tsunamis. The energy that causes them originates not at the surface, but on or below the sea bed. Tsunamis are caused by submarine earthquakes, volcanic eruptions, or the sudden sliding of huge amounts of sediment down a slope.

Movies about World War II at sea often include encounters between surface warships and submarines, in which the surface ships use depth charges. These are bombs, thrown from the ship, that explode deep below the surface. Next time you watch one of these movies, look closely at the water surface when a depth charge explodes, and you will see what looks like a tremor traveling outward as a disk. The water itself does not seem to move and there are no big waves, but the tremor is clearly visible as a whitening of the water, moving very fast. In fact, the tremor is a series of surface waves, but they are very small. Then, of course, a great gush of water is thrown into the air. The tremor is a shock wave just like the one that causes tsunamis, although much weaker; the tsunami wave it generates is very different from an ordinary wave.

Shock waves cross the ocean very fast. Typically, a tsunami travels at about 450 MPH (720 KPH); because it originates at the sea bed, it affects all of the water, not just the upper layers. The entire ocean vibrates as a tsunami passes. It is a very long wave, with a wavelength of 70–300 miles, or 112–480 kilometers (the distance from one wavecrest to the next); therefore it also has a long period, with up to 20 minutes elapsing between the passage of one wavecrest and the next. The long wavelength means the "particles" of water disturbed by the waves describe much bigger circles than those of other waves, sometimes with a diameter of 30 feet (9 meters). The wave height, on the other hand, is tiny, just like those in the tremor caused by a subsurface explosion. Usually these waves are no more than 3 feet (90 centimeters) high, and often less. They have not the slightest effect on ships, and sailors seldom even notice them.

Figure 18: *Water movement beneath waves.*

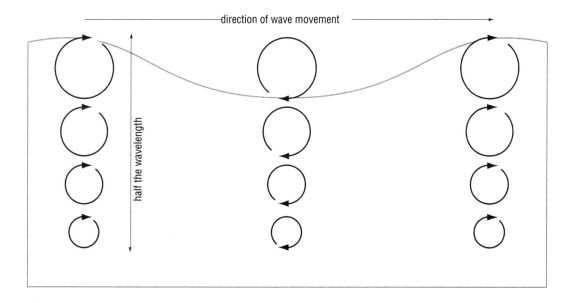

direction of wave movement

half the wavelength

This is how they travel across the open sea, but their behavior starts to change as they enter shallower water. The tsunami that struck Hawaii in 1946 was watched by the captain of a ship moored out at sea, in deep water. The wave passed his ship, but he did not feel it.

As the height of the sea bed increases, the circles described by the "particles" of water near the bottom are flattened. This slows the wave, but more waves continue to arrive at the same speed from farther out at sea, so the wave period remains the same. The same amount of energy is moving; if the waves at the front are slowing down, the energy carrying them forward is translated into making them higher. Wave height increases and, because the tsunami is traveling so fast, the wave can grow very high indeed. When the wavelength has been reduced to 5 miles, the wave at the front will be about 10 feet (3 meters) high. Depending on the slope of the sea bed, at this stage the tsunami may still be a long way from the shore. Closer to shore, where the bed slopes more steeply, the wave may be slowed to no more than 20 MPH (32 KPH), but behind it the shock wave is still traveling at 450 MPH (720 KPH) and water literally piles up.

As the wave height increases and the wavelength decreases, the waves become steeper. At the same time, the water particles move faster in their circles. The "particles" at the crest of the wave may move faster than the wave itself, but in the same direction. When this happens, water spills from the front of the wave, producing a breaker.

Tsunamis sometimes arrive as a huge, plunging breaker, which is how they are usually portrayed in movies. You might wonder why anyone would call what looks like a huge breaker a "tidal wave," and you would be right. Most tsunamis do not arrive as breakers. Even close to shore, their wavelengths are so long they are more like an incoming tide that rises and then goes on rising, much faster than a real tide and, of course, to a much higher level.

When a tsunami appears as a single huge breaker, it is merely a foretaste, running ahead of the main wave. That will arrive a few minutes later, and will be much bigger.

After the tsunami has rushed inland, the water subsides and flows back into the sea. The volume of water is huge, and as it flows seaward it meets the next wave. The collision slows the incoming wave and makes it even larger.

Tsunamis are not all the same size. The greater the magnitude of the sea bed event that caused them, the bigger they will be, and as the shock wave spreads, it also weakens. Friction in the water dissipates its energy, and the farther it travels from the source of the disturbance, the greater the area over which its energy is spread.

Throw a stone into the center of a big enough pond, and the ripples may die away before reaching the bank.

At present, scientists know too little about the ocean floor to provide accurate, reliable warnings, but the situation is improving as more instruments are installed to detect the changes associated with tsunamis. The Tsunami Warning System, in which 26 nations collaborate, covers the Pacific with a network of stations monitoring the ocean floor and waters. The National Oceanic and Atmospheric Administration (NOAA) operates two warning stations, at Palmer, Alaska, covering the west coast of Canada and the United States, and the Pacific Tsunami Warning Center at Ewa Beach, Hawaii. Tahiti is the site of the Centre Polynésien de Prévention des Tsunamis. If a tsunami is detected, the authorities are notified. They issue warnings, as do the NOAA Weather Radio System and the U.S. Coast Guard.

Meanwhile, if you live near the coast, there are signs you can watch for yourself. Ordinarily, waves break on the shore, then rush back into the sea. If, for no apparent reason, the water retreats much farther than usual, exposing rocks that normally remain covered even at spring tides, you should beware. A few minutes later the water will return, rising much higher up the shore than it did before and remaining there for several minutes before flowing back into the sea. If the water rises more than 3 feet (90 centimeters) beyond its normal level, remains there for a few minutes, then retreats to more than 3 feet below its normal level, you have been warned. You should move immediately to high ground inland and warn everyone else. Do not wait to collect possessions. Some miles away out at sea, but approaching fast, there is a tsunami. Eventually you will see it as a wall of water on the horizon, but by then it may be too late to escape. Within just a few minutes its full force will arrive.

Along the coast of Oregon and Washington, Native Americans have a legend about a huge flood that swept inland one cold winter night when the ground shook. A year or two ago, Japanese scientists checked the legend against old records in their own country and found reports of a tsunami, 7–10 feet (2.1–3.0 meters) high, that flooded rice fields and a storehouse and damaged houses at around midnight on January 27, 1700. There was no record of an earthquake associated with this tsunami, but the scientists were able to check records from many other parts of the world. Eventually they identified the culprit: a massive earthquake just off the coast of Oregon, Washington, and British Columbia that happened at 9:00 P.M. on January 26, 1700, just as the local legend describes. Not only did the research show that the legend was based on fact, but it implied a warning. That earthquake was a giant, much bigger than any the region has experienced in modern times, and it could happen again. If it did, rocks might rupture along a 600-mile

(960-kilometer) belt, and the tsunamis might be more than 60 feet (18 meters) high.

Tsunamis are one more hazard to which people living along coasts, especially Pacific coasts, are exposed. As with flash floods, it is their habit of striking suddenly and with devastating force that makes them terrifying.

Tides

Twice every day the sea rises to cover part of the shore, and twice every day it recedes again. This is flooding, but it is so ordinary that no one thinks of it in this way. Occasionally, though, other factors may add to this regular movement; then there can be real and severe flooding extending some distance inland (see page 64).

The regular rise and fall of the sea is due to the tides. It is not the same everywhere. In some places, 2 high tides occur 12 hours apart, but in parts of the China Sea they sometimes occur more than 24 hours apart. There are places, such as Southampton, England, where high tide is followed by a small ebb and then a second high tide.

Usually, the tide ebbs to about the same distance as it rises, but the size and timing of the tides vary day by day, and some coasts experience much bigger tides than others. Along Mediterranean shores, for example, tidal movements are very small, seldom exceeding 2 feet (60 centimeters). At London Bridge, some distance inland on the tidal Thames, the average tidal movement is about 15 feet (450 centimeters), and it sometimes reaches 21 feet (630 centimeters). In the Bay of Fundy, on the Canadian east coast, the tide sometimes rises more than 50 feet (15 meters). All bodies of water have tides, but in any body smaller than a large sea, the effect is too small to be noticed.

Clearly, tides are complicated, but their underlying cause is fairly simple. They are produced by the combined effects of the rotation of the Earth and the gravitational attraction of the Moon and Sun. Swing a bucket of water in a circle, and the water will not spill, because once a body is set in motion it tends to continue moving in a straight line, so the water in the bucket tends to move away from you. This tendency of any body to resist changes to its state of rest or motion is called "inertia." The rope by which the bucket of water is swinging prevents it from flying away by exerting a force, called "centripetal force," in the opposite direction. Provided the centripetal force is equal to or greater than the inertial force, the bucket will continue to swing, but should the inertial force exceed the centripetal force, the rope will break and the bucket will escape.

The Earth spins on its axis; the water in the oceans is like the bucket of water. It has inertia, which tends to push it off into space in a straight line at a tangent (a line at right angles to the radius and touching the circumference at one point) to the circumference of the Earth. In this case it is the gravitational attraction of the Earth that exerts the centripetal force, and this is strong enough to prevent us from losing all our oceans into space. The gravitational centripetal force is strong enough to hold the oceans, but their inertia acting in the opposite direction reduces their weight. Consequently, the oceans bulge outward. Their bulge is biggest around the equator, because that is where they are traveling fastest (any point on the equator must travel faster than any point North or South of the equator in order to complete a full rotation each day) and, therefore, their inertial force is greatest.

The Moon and Sun also exert a gravitational pull. Like the inertial force due to the Earth's rotation, this also reduces the weight of the oceans and increases the size of the bulge. Although the Sun is much bigger than the Moon, it is also much more distant, so its gravitational influence is much smaller; it is mainly the Moon that is responsible for tides.

In fact, there are two bulges. As figure 19 shows, with the shaded areas indicating the bulges, at the point on the surface of the Earth directly facing the Moon, the gravitational pull from the Moon draws up one bulge. On the other side of the Earth, at the point directly opposite the Moon, the attraction of the Moon is insignificant, and the inertial force is much greater, producing the second bulge.

These bulges are both the same size, because the gravitational attraction between two bodies (in this case, the Earth and the Moon) is proportional to their masses and the distance between them, and it draws together the centers of both bodies. All the water in all the oceans is drawn by gravity toward the center of the Earth. The Moon offsets this attraction by an amount proportional to the distance from the center of the Moon to the Earth's surface to the Earth's center. The distance between the Earth's surface and its center, one Earth radius, is the same for the point directly beneath the Moon and the point on the other side of the world directly opposite. Directly beneath the Moon its attraction is greatest proportional to one Earth radius and on the opposite of the Earth it is least, proportional to one Earth radius. At every other point on the surface, water is drawn by smaller forces toward the nearer bulge.

As the Moon circles the Earth, taking 24 hours, 50 minutes, and 28 seconds to complete each orbit, the two bulges follow it. Essentially, that is what produces two tides a day, 12 hours, 25 minutes, and 14 seconds apart. This is called the "equilibrium tide," and it is what would happen if the entire Earth were covered by oceans and the Moon was always directly overhead at the equator.

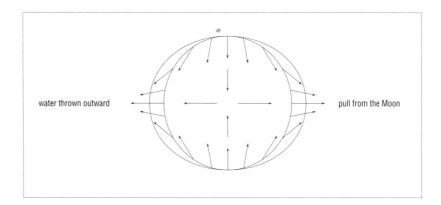

water thrown outward

pull from the Moon

Figure 19: *Pulls that produce tides.*

Obviously, neither is true, and so the real situation is more complicated. The tilt of the Earth's axis means the Moon is sometimes to the north of the equator and sometimes to the south by up to 28.5°. This displaces the tidal bulge and, therefore, the magnitude of the tides changes from day to day. If the tidal bulge were to remain directly beneath the Moon and the point opposite, it would have to move as a wave in water about 12 miles (19.2 kilometers) deep. The oceans are much shallower than this, and their friction with the ocean bed slows the wave, so it lags behind the position of the Moon.

Although the Moon is the more important influence, the Sun also exerts a gravitational pull on the oceans, producing tidal bulges like those produced by the Moon, but smaller. The Sun and Moon do not always pull in the same direction, however. Sometimes the Sun pulls against the Moon and makes the tides smaller; sometimes both pull together to make them larger. Tides reach their maximum height at spring tides and are at their lowest at neap tides.

At the time of spring tides, the Moon and Sun are aligned. When the Moon is new, it lies almost directly between the Earth and Sun, so the two tidal pulls act in the same direction and the bulges combine. When the Moon is full, the Moon, Earth, and Sun are also aligned, but this time the Moon is on the side of the Earth opposite the Sun. The bulge on the side of the Earth opposite the point directly beneath the Sun is in the same place as the bulge directly beneath the Moon, so again the tides are high.

Neap tides occur when the pulls of the Sun and Moon act at right angles to one another. This happens at the first and third quarters of the Moon. Figure 20 illustrates the alignments for spring and neap tides.

All this would be fine if there were no continents, but there are and they have coastlines aligned in every direction, with headlands, bays, and offshore islands. The tidal bulges move around the Earth like waves (in this case, true tidal waves), but coastlines deflect and reflect them and, like other waves, their characteristics change when they move from deep to shallow water (see page 58). In small seas almost enclosed by land, tidal waves may enter from more than one direction, meet, and then move back and forth in a complicated manner. This happens in the North Sea, for example, where tides from the Atlantic enter in the north, around the north coast of Scotland, and in the south, through the English Channel and the Straits of Dover.

Coastlines are seldom aligned at right angles to the tidal waves, so the tides reach one part of the coast first, then travel along it as a current flowing parallel to the coast. This is a "longshore current," and a curve in the coastline can deflect it back out to sea as a "rip current." Such currents are common and make it very dangerous to bathe or surf on certain parts of many beaches. They also explain why the times of high and low tides are different along different parts of the same coastline.

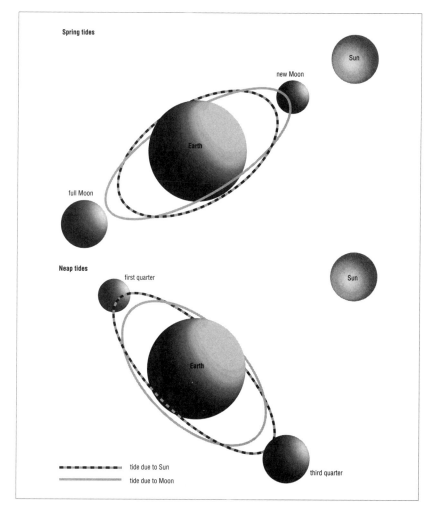

Figure 20: *Spring and neap tides.*

When the tidal wave approaches the shore, it enters shallow water and, as with any other kind of wave, its wave height increases. The waves flow with some force up the beach and, as they return, can carry with them material from sandy or gravel beaches that has been disturbed by their turbulence.

Longshore currents can then remove this material and deposit it elsewhere. The process is called "littoral drift." This results in coastal erosion in some places and extensions of the coast in others. Of course, it is also waves, generated by wind and tides, that form beaches in the first place by constantly battering coastal rocks until boulders break away from them and are then slowly reduced to small pebbles or sand. Waves may also move material higher up the beach. This sand or gravel may then accumulate along a line marking the highest point strong waves commonly reach, making a ridge called a "berm." Berms can be quite high, and they shelter the land behind them, making it an apparently attractive place to build. It is not always a wise place to build, however. The sea that built the berm can just as easily demolish it, and it can do so in the course of a single storm.

Tidal surges

Think of a hurricane, and the first image that springs to mind is of the fierce wind. Hurricanes are winds of terrifying force, of course, and they can cause great damage. It is not usually the wind that does most harm, however, but water. Storms deliver heavy rain, which can cause flash floods (see page 48), but they also produce storm surges, sending the sea crashing through coastal communities. When Hurricane Fran struck Cape Fear, North Carolina, and then moved northward along the coast on September 6, 1996, the wind and rain were accompanied by a storm surge of 12 feet (3.6 meters) and, in some places, 16 feet (4.8 meters).

Fran was a big hurricane, but typical of many, and its storm surge was no bigger than those produced by earlier hurricanes. Hurricane Opal, which crossed the coast of the southeastern United States in October 1995, for example, caused a 12-foot (3.6-meter) storm surge, and in 1992 Tropical Storm Polly produced a storm surge of 20 feet (6 meters) at Tianjin, in southeastern China.

A hurricane, which scientists call a "tropical cyclone," is an intense depression, or region of low atmospheric pressure. Depressions, which meteorologists call "cyclones," are familiar in middle latitudes. They usually travel from west to east, bringing low clouds and rain or snow, sometimes with strong winds. They are associated with bad weather, but not dangerous weather, and some are so weak they do not even produce many clouds or much precipitation. Nevertheless, the atmospheric pressure at a depression's center is lower than that away from the center. They are "lows."

Tropical cyclones are also depressions, but on a much bigger scale. This means that as one forms the pressure at its center falls much further than it would in a mild midlatitude depression. The average atmospheric pressure at sea level is 1,013 millibars (mb). In the eye of a category 1 hurricane, which is the gentlest type of tropical cyclone, the pressure is 980 mb or lower. Hurricane Fran, which caused serious damage in the Carolinas, Virginia, and West Virginia, was a category 3 hurricane. It produced steady winds of 115 MPH (184 KPH), and the pressure at its center was between 945 and 964 mb.

This is a drop in pressure of no more than 5 to 7 percent. This drop is quite small, but its consequences are not. Atmospheric pressure is due to the weight of all the air, right to the top of the atmosphere, pressing down on a surface (see box on page 66). When the water is still, the surface of a small pond is absolutely level. You can see reflections in it. This is because the air is pressing down on it to the same extent everywhere.

Suppose, though, that there was a little less air over one small part of the pond. You could measure this as a lower atmospheric pressure. If there is less air, and the pressure is lower, the air is pressing less heavily on that part of the surface, so the water will rise a little. In fact, a drop in pressure of 1 mb will allow the water to rise about 0.4 inch (1 centimeter).

At the center of a tropical cyclone, the fall in pressure is much greater than this. Hurricane Fran had an eye pressure 49–68 mb below the average sea-level pressure. This would allow the water beneath the eye to rise 19–27 inches (48.3–68.6 centimeters).

Since we think of water as "finding its own level," it seems that, except for waves, the surface of open water should be absolutely level. However, some parts of the sea surface are higher than others. Weather satellites use radar to measure how the height of the sea surface varies from place to place, because these variations allow the surface atmospheric pressure to be calculated.

Sea level will rise due only to a fall in atmospheric pressure at the surface; for example, when a tropical cyclone crosses a coast the sea may rise about 2 feet (60 centimeters). This may not be very important in itself, but suppose it happens at high tide or, even worse, at the height of a spring tide. Then this small rise might be enough to flow over the top of a sea wall.

This is not the only potential effect of a difference in atmospheric pressure; such a difference will also cause air to flow as wind, spiraling into the low-pressure center with a force proportional to

Air pressure, highs and lows

When air is warmed, it expands and becomes less dense. When air is chilled, it contracts and becomes more dense.

Air expands by pushing away the air around it. It rises because it is less dense than the air immediately above it. Air flows in to

Pressure gradient and wind speed (pressures in millibars).

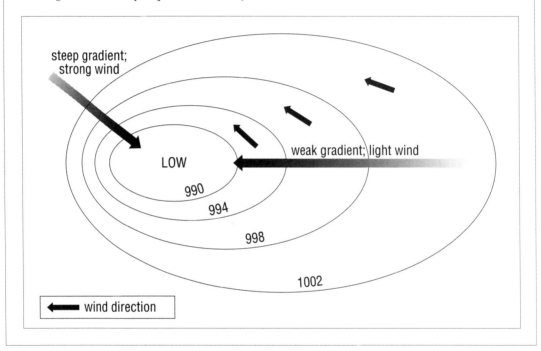

steep gradient; strong wind

LOW

weak gradient; light wind

990

994

998

1002

◄— wind direction

the difference in pressure inside and outside the low. It is the large pressure difference that causes the hurricane winds. At sea, winds also produce waves. A sustained wind of more than 110 MPH (176 KPH) will generate waves more than 30 feet (9 meters) high. These waves move away from their source with a fairly long period (see page 55); as they slow down, they are overtaken by more waves moving faster. If several waves combine, the waves will grow even bigger.

Both the sea-level rise due to low pressure and the wind-generated waves contribute to the storm surge. When a surge is forecast, its height is given as the amount by which the sea will rise above the predicted high tide on an open coast. In a sheltered bay or estuary (the lowest part of a river, where it meets the sea and its level rises and falls as tidal water flows upstream, then ebbs toward the sea), the rise may be half as great again.

Storm surges are not confined to those parts of the world affected by tropical cyclones. At Woolwich, downstream from the center of replace it, is warmed by contact with the surface, and also expands and rises. If you imagine a column of air extending all the way from the surface to the top of the atmosphere, warming from below causes air to be pushed out of the column, so it contains less air (fewer molecules of air) than it did when it was cooler. Because there is less air in the column, the pressure its weight exerts at the surface is reduced. The result is an area of low surface pressure, often called simply a "low."

In chilled air, the opposite happens. The air molecules move closer together, so the air contracts, becomes more dense, and sinks. The amount of air in the column increases, its weight increases, and the surface atmospheric pressure also increases. This produces an area of high pressure, or simply a "high."

At sea level, the atmosphere exerts sufficient pressure to raise a column of mercury about 30 inches (760 mm) in a tube from which the air has been removed. Meteorologists call this pressure one "bar" and measure atmospheric pressure in "millibars" (1,000 millibar [mb] = 1 bar = 10^6 dynes cm^{-2} = 101 325 pascals).

Air pressure decreases with height, because there is less weight of air above to exert pressure. Pressure measured at different places on the surface is corrected to sea-level pressure, to remove differences due only to altitude. Lines are then drawn, linking places where the pressure is the same. These lines, called "isobars," allow meteorologists to study the distribution of pressure.

Like water flowing downhill, air flows from high to low pressure. Its speed, which we feel as wind strength, depends on the difference in pressure between the two regions. This is called the "pressure gradient." On a weather map, it is calculated from the distance between isobars, just as the distance between contours on an ordinary map allows the steepness of hills to be measured. The steeper the gradient, the stronger the wind.

Moving air experiences friction with the surface. This slows it more over land, where the friction is greater, than over the sea. It is also subject to the Coriolis effect, which swings it to the right in the northern hemisphere and to the left in the southern hemisphere. As a consequence, winds do not cross the isobars at 90°. Over the oceans they cross at about 30°, and over land at about 45°.

London, there is an array of floodgates called the Thames Barrier, constructed in 1982 to protect London from flooding due to storm surges. There have been several storm surges: one of the most serious occurred in 1953, when the sea level at Southend, on the coast, rose 9 feet (2.7 meters) 2.5 hours before high tide; at high tide it was still 5.5 feet (1.7 meters) above its normal level. This surge traveled around the North Sea, causing damage and loss of life in England and the Netherlands.

Tides and surges both move around the North Sea in a counterclockwise direction. Tidal water enters from the Atlantic in the north and south, so two tides flow in opposite directions and meet. This might set up a complicated oscillation of water sloshing back and forth, but tidal movement is affected by the rotation of the Earth (the Coriolis effect), resulting in the counterclockwise flow around three centers, called "amphidromic points," where there is no tidal movement at all. One amphidromic point is halfway between the east coast of England and the Netherlands, the second in the northern part of the German Bight, opposite Denmark, and the third close to the southern coast of Norway. If a deep depression crosses the northern part of the sea, producing a gale blowing from the north, it can generate long-period waves traveling around the sea, while the low pressure also raises the sea level. When these combine with the tidal flow, the resulting surge can be large.

Tides cause the sea level to rise, but in a regular, predictable way. Storms also cause the sea level to rise, because of the reduction in atmospheric pressure at their centers. Storms also produce wind-generated waves. When the rise in sea level due to a storm coincides with high tide, the result is a surge of water that can flow over coasts with great force.

Coastal erosion

After a certain stormy night a year or two ago, a couple who had recently moved into a house beside the north shore of the Firth of Forth, in eastern Scotland, found that half of their backyard had disappeared into the sea, leaving a large hole filled with sea water. A sea wall, built many years ago and thought to be safe, had been breached by the waves.

Hundreds of miles away, on a different coast and at a different time, the grounds of a hotel vanished when the cliff beneath them collapsed. The building had become so insecure that the emergency services allowed the owners of the hotel 10 minutes to remove their belongings.

Entire villages that were once beside the sea are now beneath it, some distance from the shore. Other villages that once had harbors and fishing fleets are now a mile or more inland.

Coasts change constantly. Some scientists define "coast" as a wide belt of land and sea, in which the shoreline shifts back and forth. These shifts occur naturally, but several different forces are involved, and not all shorelines are affected to the same degree.

Part of this change is due to the fact that in some places the land itself is still rising and in others sinking as a result of the melting of the glaciers and ice sheets at the end of the last ice age. Ice is heavy, and an ice sheet thousands of feet thick is very heavy indeed. It presses down on the rocks beneath it. These rocks, in turn, rest on the hot, slightly plastic rock of the mantle below the solid rocks of the Earth's crust, and the extra weight of the ice makes them sink into it. At the edges of glaciers and ice sheets where the ice is thinner, however, the ice pushes upward as it meets and is shaped by surface resistance, carrying rocks with it, so the center of the ice sits in a depression and its edges on a bulge. When the ice age ends and the ice melts, the weight is removed, and very slowly the rocks return to their former level. Figure 22 shows the result. Rocks that were beneath the center of an ice sheet rise; those that were near the edges sink. This readjustment, called "glacioisostasy," began as the ice retreated around 10,000 years ago and it has not yet been completed. In Scandinavia, the weight of the ice depressed the land by about 3,000 feet (900 meters); so far it has risen again by about 1,700 feet (510 meters). In parts of Scotland there are beaches, with seashells embedded in them, that are 130 feet (3.9 meters) above the present sea level. Northeastern Canada, Greenland, northern Scandinavia, and northern Scotland are rising, so there the sea level is falling. Elsewhere around the coasts of North America and Europe, the land is sinking and sea levels are rising.

This sea-level rise due to the glacioisostatic sinking of the land increases the risk of coastal flooding along much of the eastern seaboard of the United States and on coasts bordering the southern North Sea. Eastern and southeastern England are vulnerable, which was part of the reason for building the Thames Barrier (see page 67) to protect London from tidal surges. Obviously, the risk is greatest where coastal land is low-lying. London averages 16 feet (4.9 meters) above sea level, but parts are lower, and severe

Figure 21: *Cueva del Indio, an eroded sea cave on the coast of Puerto Rico at Arecibo.* (U.S. Geological Survey/W. H. Munroe)

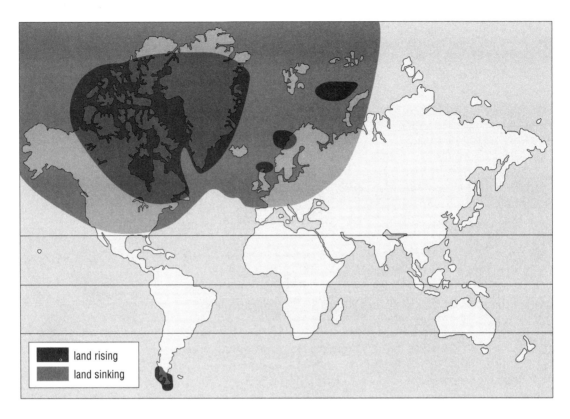

land rising
land sinking

Figure 22: *Land adjustments following the last ice age.*

flooding could swamp the subways and sewers, with disastrous consequences. Some American cities are also at risk. Baltimore is only 14 feet (4.2 meters) above sea level; Charleston, South Carolina, 9 feet (2.7 meters); Miami, 25 feet (7.5 meters); and Norfolk, Virginia, 11 feet (3.3 meters).

Over the past century, the average temperature has risen slightly throughout the world. This has warmed the oceans and when water is warmed, it expands. The oceans have expanded, and this has raised the sea level by about 6 inches (15.24 centimeters) compared with its level around 1900. If global warming continues, the sea level is expected to go on rising, due to the combined effects of thermal expansion and the melting of glaciers, by about 0.8–1.5 inches (2.0–3.8 centimeters) every 10 years. The rise is small, but it could make floods more frequent along very low-lying coasts, especially coasts that are sinking due to glacioisostatic readjustment, in other words, submerged under the weight of glacial ice.

These changes happen so slowly no one notices them. Along some coasts, where storms and surging waves seem to be growing bigger or more frequent, sea walls are made higher and stronger, but elsewhere vulnerable coasts are considered very attractive places to live.

Other changes are wrought by the sea itself. Sea cliffs were once rounded hills. Continual battering by waves wears away the rocks of which they are made, cutting them back and leaving the sheer faces we see today. This process never ceases. Walk along the beach at the foot of a cliff after a storm, and you will often see boulders recently torn from the cliff. Eventually, the sea and wind will break them apart again and again until they are reduced to gravel or sand.

A sea wall can protect a cliff against erosion by waves; many such walls have been built, especially in places where the cliff is only a few feet high and there are roads and buildings close to its edge. Often sea walls succeed, but they can fail. It was the failure of an apparently secure sea wall that carried away part of the backyard overlooking the Firth of Forth. If the beach between the wall and the sea is low enough for waves to break against the wall itself, the reflection of the waves from the wall will scour away the beach. This lowers the beach still further and exposes more of the wall. Lowering the height of the beach reduces the amount of energy that waves dissipate crossing it, so the waves have more energy when they strike the wall. In time, this can weaken the wall.

The best protection for a cliff is a high beach. This was demonstrated dramatically in south Devon, England. In 1887, about 725,000 tons (797,500 tonnes) of shingle were mined from a beach there to be used as building material for the construction of new dockyards at Plymouth. This reduced the height of the beach by about 13 feet (3.9 meters) and allowed waves to break with full force against the cliff behind the beach. Between 1907 and 1957 the cliff retreated by 20 feet (6 meters). Waves then attacked the village of Hallsand, by then on the clifftop, eventually leaving it in ruins.

Coasts where there are beaches made from sand or gravel are the most popular places to vacation and to live. They are also the most changeable. How quickly they change depends on the configuration of the coastline and the character of the sea to which they are exposed. There are "high-energy" coastlines and "low-energy" coastlines. You can tell one from the other by looking at a map. A high-energy coastline will be very irregular in shape, with cliffs, headlands, bays, and small coves, or with sand dunes and big, sandy beaches. A low-energy coastline will be generally low-lying and straighter, with wide, shallow bays and spits projecting from it here and there.

It is easy to imagine how waves erode coastlines, but they also build them. Material removed by the sea from one place is usually deposited somewhere else.

As a wave approaches a beach, it enters increasingly shallow water and eventually breaks (see page 58), then spills up the beach and expends the last of its energy, with water falling over itself repeatedly. This turbulence stirs up the sand or gravel, and as the water flows back down the beach and toward the sea some of this material travels with it, only to be carried back by the next breaking wave. If the waves were generated by winds far out at sea, they reach the shore quite widely separated, as a regular swell. Ocean swell tends to carry material onto the beach and leave it there, so it builds beaches. Storms close to the shore produce short, steep waves that carry material away from the beach. Many beaches are eroded by storms, then rebuilt by the ocean swell between storms; although they are constantly changing, it is around an average, and in time building and erosion balance. Often, the balance takes place over the year. Winter storms erode the beach, so in spring it is quite small, but calmer weather in the summer and fall restore it.

Fine sand grains are easier to shift than are large grains or pebbles. One consequence of this is that the larger particles tend to be pushed up the beach rather than carried into the sea. Generally, this means that the bigger the particles from which the beach is made, the steeper it will be.

Waves seldom arrive at right angles to a coast. Most of the time they strike obliquely. This produces a "longshore current," flowing parallel to the shore. As each wave breaks at an angle, beach material is carried up the beach at one angle, then down the beach at another angle, and some of it is caught in the longshore current. Both on the beach and in the water adjacent to it, sand and even gravel are carried along the coast. The process is called "littoral drift" (the word *littoral* is from *Littorina littorea*, the edible periwinkle, which is common along many coasts). Figure 23 shows how littoral drift, produced by wind- and tide-generated waves, shifts beach material along the coast. The wavy line represents the direction in which material is transported by wave action, the parallel lines the longshore current into which some of the material is swept. The process works steadily, but a brief increase in wave energy can accelerate it dramatically, and a substantial part of a beach can vanish overnight.

Farther along, where the angle between the shoreline and the waves is different, the current loses energy and drops the material it is carrying. There it accumulates, eventually building into a bar or barrier.

Littoral drift has alarming implications for people living beside beaches, so it is not surprising that they try to prevent it. It is not only shoreline property that is at risk. The beach itself may be a valuable asset, attracting vacationers, and as seaside holidays became popular in the last century, attempts were made to prevent the disappearance of beaches that attracted visitors with money to spend. Groins were a favorite device. Some are still in place, and the remains of others can be seen on many beaches.

A groin is like a sea wall, but erected at right angles to the shore, so it lies across the beach, extending as far as the low-tide mark or beyond. Often groins were made from timber. Their purpose is to trap the sand or gravel carried by waves before it can move far enough off-shore to become littoral drift.

Groins are rarely used nowadays, because after they had been in place for some years, it was found they had curious effects. As the upper drawing in figure 24 shows, in the absence of groins, littoral drift transports material along the beach at the base of the cliffs. Build a groin and it will capture much of this material, as shown in the lower drawing. This is what it is meant to do, of course, but the groin breaks the waves. This sends water eddying turbulently around the other side of the groin, adding to the force of the waves there, so it reduces beach erosion on one side, but increases it on the other. A series of groins along a beach eventually alters the shape of the beach to one with triangular heaps of sand or gravel against one side of each groin and a scooped-out, much smaller beach between groins. More seriously, reducing parts of the beach in this way accelerates the erosion of the cliff behind the beach.

Piers and jetties, projecting into the water at right angles to the shoreline, have a similar effect. They, too, can accumulate beach material on one side and accelerate erosion on the other. Beaches move about naturally, and in most cases it is probably wise to let them do so.

Along much of the eastern seaboard of the United States, the high-energy coast is protected by barrier islands. These are made from sand scoured from the coast by waves and then deposited as

Figure 23: *Transport of material by littoral drift.*

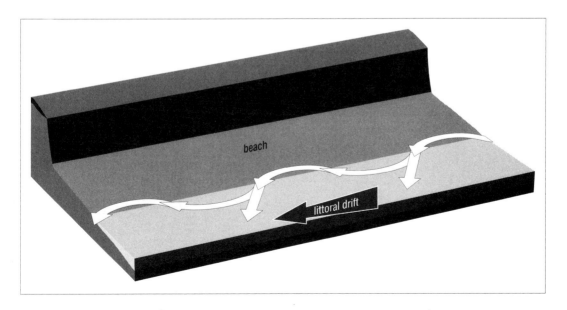

long strips lying parallel to the shore. Waves sweep right over the
lower barrier islands, and the higher barrier islands often have wide
beaches. They absorb the energy of the waves and, in doing so,
they constantly change shape and location. Damaging the barrier
islands can quickly expose the coast to the full force of the waves,
so care is taken to protect them. Even this can cause problems,
however. In the 1930s, some of the barrier islands off the North
Carolina coast were protected by sand fencing, built to trap sand
and prevent it from being swept away during storms. The sand
dunes grew taller, and plants were established to stabilize them.
Waves could no longer lose their energy gradually by flowing over
and between unstable dunes. Instead, they expended energy all at
once on the permanent dunes. The beaches over which the waves
flowed became narrower and steeper, erosion increased, and

behind the islands water driven into Pamlico Sound by northeasterly winds could no longer drain across the islands to the sea, so now it accumulates and floods the coastal area.

Large rivers also extend coastlines and protect them from erosion and flooding. Rivers carry soil particles eroded from land all along their courses. As they flow into the sea, chemical reactions between the chlorine in sea water and the particles cause them to cling together in lumps (the process is called "flocculation"), which settle to the bottom. Gradually this sediment grows thicker until it is capable of absorbing a substantial part of the energy of waves crossing it. In some places the sediment lies so close to the surface that the land can be reclaimed from the sea.

Inland, however, soil erosion from farmland is a serious problem (see page 85), and great efforts have been made to reduce it. These efforts have been successful, but reducing erosion means the rivers no longer carry so much soil. Between the 1930s and 1960s, the amount of soil transported by the four principal rivers of Texas (the Brazos, San Bernard, Colorado, and Rio Grande) fell by 80 percent. There has also been a large reduction in material carried by the Mississippi. This has reduced the volume of sediment deposited in the Gulf of Mexico and increased coastal erosion. Over the last century, Texas has lost four times more land along its coast than it has gained by reclamation, which is due partly to the success of its soil conservation policies inland. River discharges have been reduced in this way along the Atlantic coast of the United States.

Most of us enjoy walking and playing on the beach. The sea attracts many people and, not surprisingly, some choose to live there. If they relocate to a stretch of low-energy coast, where the sea is gentle, all may be well, but high-energy coasts can be dangerous places, where the shoreline moves back and forth, cliffs collapse, new land emerges from the sea, and flooding can occur at any time.

The cost of floods

Salt Water Infiltration

Some years ago, the Dutch authorities deliberately allowed some of the fields bordering the North Sea to be flooded with fresh water to hold back the sea. They feared a rise in the sea level would cause salt water to infiltrate below ground, contaminating the groundwater. Had this happened and been allowed to continue, the contamination might have affected a large area. In time it would have made the soil infertile.

Most crop plants are very intolerant of salt. Plants absorb water through the tips of their root hairs. Along with it, they also absorb mineral nutrients dissolved in the water in the soil. This soil solution is more diluted than the solution inside the plant, so it passes readily through the cell walls of the root hairs by osmosis (see box on page 77). For most plants (some are adapted to salt water), this works only if the soil solution is based on fresh water. The presence of salt makes the solution more concentrated, and water does not need to be very salty before it is more concentrated than the solution inside cells. In that case, osmotic pressure causes water to move in the opposite direction, out of the cell. This is why if you drink only sea water you will become increasingly thirsty as the cells of your body lose water and dehydrate, and it is why most plants die in salt water and salt renders soils infertile.

The Dutch remedy was to seal off coastal polders on the landward side and flood them with fresh water to keep out the salt water. What were once fields are now freshwater lakes. As an amenity they are valuable, but making them has required the loss of farmland. This was a deliberate manipulation of flooding. Causing a flood at the surface prevented a much more serious flood below ground.

Polders are fields made by reclaiming land from the sea. The Netherlands is famous for them; the word itself is of Dutch origin. People who settled on the river deltas and along the adjacent, low-lying, marshy coast of what is now the Netherlands were at constant risk from floods. As early as the 1st century they were building mounds to protect their land from the rivers as well as the sea, and the first dikes may have been built in the 8th or 9th century. By the end of the 13th century entire areas of farmland were enclosed by dikes; more have been added, and more land reclaimed, in the centuries since then. Between 1920 and 1932, part of the Zuider Zee was closed, giving the country more than half a million acres of additional farmland. The Dutch polders now occupy 2,500 square miles (6,500 square kilometers), almost one-fifth of the total land area of the Netherlands; much of this land lies below sea level. Prins Alexander Polder, the lowest point in the country, is 22 feet (6.6 meters) below sea level.

The Dutch are especially renowned for their land reclamation, but people have been reclaiming land from the sea throughout history, and no doubt were doing so before anyone compiled written records. Today there are polders in many countries, wherever coastal lands are flat and low-lying and farmland is in short supply. There are polders in England, France, Germany, Denmark, Japan, India, Guinea, Venezuela, and many other countries. In the

Osmosis

Certain membranes are partially permeable: Some molecules can pass through them, but not others. Many biological membranes are of this type, but they can also be manufactured industrially.

If a partially permeable membrane separates two solutions of different strengths, a pressure across the membrane will force solvent molecules from the weaker to the stronger solution until both are at the same strength. This is called "osmotic pressure," and the process by which molecules cross the membrane under osmotic pressure is called "osmosis." The most common naturally occurring solutions are of substances dissolved in water, so the movement across membranes is most commonly of water.

Cells are enclosed within partially permeable membranes and contain substances dissolved in water. If the solution outside the cell is stronger than that inside, water will pass out of the cell. If the solution inside the cell is stronger, water will pass into the cell.

18th century there were polders in Georgia and the Carolinas, used mainly for growing rice (see page 40), but eventually these fell into disuse and the land reverted to coastal marsh.

To make a polder, the first step is to surround the area with dikes. These are levees (see page 104) high and strong enough to keep out the sea. Then the water must be removed. If the polder is above the high-tide level, surface water can be allowed to drain away at low tide, and the polder resealed. If the polder lies below the low-tide level, the water must be removed by pumping. That is the purpose of the windmills for which the Netherlands is famous. Windmills lifted water from the polders and poured it into elevated drainage channels that carried it to the sea. The windmills remaining today are there as tourist attractions. Engines now drive the pumps that do the real work.

Once the surface water has been drained away, the salt must be removed from the soil. This is done by pumping fresh water, or water containing very little salt, onto the surface. As the water sinks through the soil, the salts dissolve into the water and are carried into the drainage system and away to the sea. In time, a layer of fresh water accumulates below ground and joins the groundwater draining from farther inland. Fresh water is less dense than salt water and lies above it. A boundary forms between the fresh and salt water, with a layer of fresh water deep enough to supply the needs of the farmer. As soon as the soil has been treated to make it fertile, the polder is ready for use.

Below ground and within the reach of plant roots, there is fresh groundwater. On the seaward side, however, salt water pushes some distance inland. It is denser than the fresh water, so it moves beneath it, usually as a wedge. As the upper drawing in figure 25 shows, this may make the land immediately adjacent to the sea infertile, because there the groundwater is wholly salt, but a little way inland plants have adequate access to fresh water. If irrigation is needed, a well sunk into the groundwater will prove satisfactory.

It may be, though, that so much fresh water is abstracted that the water table falls, as in the lower drawing. This allows the salt water to intrude further, because there is less fresh water holding it back. It soaks into the underlying sand, gravel, or rock that formerly held fresh water. Now the well is tapping salt water, and the coastal strip made infertile by salt water below ground is wider.

The drawing suggests a sharp boundary between fresh and salt water. In fact the two mix, and the line in the drawing represents a midpoint. Moving from left to right in the drawing, the fresh water becomes a little salty, then increasingly so until it is pure sea water. Water is considered unfit to drink if its salt content exceeds 2 percent, so it takes only mild contamination to cause considerable trouble.

Figure 25: *Salt water intrusion.*

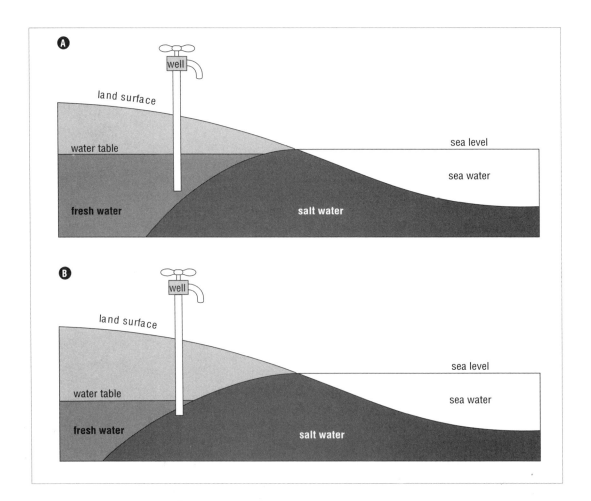

This is the problem in the Netherlands. Crop irrigation and periods of dry weather have lowered water tables, and little by little the sea is intruding into the groundwater. By flooding polders with fresh water, the intrusion of sea water is checked and the fields inland from the newly made lakes are protected.

This problem is not confined exclusively to the Netherlands. Increased water abstraction occurs when people move into an area to live; as long ago as the 1950s salt water intrusion was known to be occurring in the United States, affecting coastal areas in every state bordering the Atlantic, Pacific, and Gulf of Mexico, as well as Hawaii.

Coastal wetlands, such as marshes and mangrove forests, trap sediment and often store fresh water, but coastal development usually requires such areas to be cleared of vegetation and drained, to provide building land. This happened many years ago at Sanibel Island, a large, exposed barrier island (see page 73) off the Florida coast. Removing the vegetation led to salt water intrusion from above as well as below. Storm surges poured over the shore to cause flooding inland by salt water. Sea water also penetrated the sand dunes surrounding and protecting the interior. At the same time, salt water intruded into the groundwater.

On the mainland, canals can be built to drain surplus water from farmland and carry it toward the coast, but this can make the situation worse. In dry weather, instead of carrying fresh water seaward, sea water can push inland, so the canals flow backward and fields become contaminated by salt.

When people move into coastal areas, they need more than homes and roads. They also wish to use the sea for recreation. This sometimes calls for the digging of channels or deepening of rivers to provide sheltered anchorages linked to the open water. Sea water flows into the channels, of course, and the resulting change in the circulation of water and in its chemical composition can allow salt water to infiltrate the groundwater. When channels were cut deeper in the Sacramento River delta, that is precisely what happened.

Nor is it only the coastal strips where groundwater suffers this kind of contamination. Sea water can also move inland beneath riverbeds during dry weather, when the rivers are carrying little water. Salt water often moves beneath the Hudson as far upstream as Poughkeepsie, New York, and it also follows the Delaware, Potomac, Sacramento, and other rivers.

Salt water intrusion is a form of flooding, but one that takes place below ground and out of sight. By the time its effects become evident, the harm is done, and remedying the situation will be difficult and expensive. As always, prevention is much better than cure. In some places it is possible to insert a layer of impermeable material between the fresh and salt waters to keep them apart.

Elsewhere, sites must be examined before any development starts, to trace the way subsurface water moves, and the development planned accordingly. Wetlands (see page 99) should be disturbed as little as possible. Finally, limits should be set for the amount of fresh groundwater that can be abstracted for irrigation or other uses. If the water table is found to be falling, abstraction should be stopped and fresh water poured in to recharge the groundwater.

Flood Damage

Beneath the city streets, groundwater moves slowly downhill; at its upper margin there is a water table. Water moves below ground there as it does everywhere else, but there is an important difference. When it rains over the city, water soaks vertically downward, directly into the groundwater, only from parks, backyards, and other open spaces where there is soil and where plants grow. The rain that falls on buildings, streets, and parking lots cannot soak downward. Instead, it is carried away by drains, eventually to a river, a lake, or the sea.

Drains are pipes; there is a limit to the amount of water they can carry. Beyond a certain flow, drains can accept no more, and the water, instead of disappearing through the grills beside roads, will flow along the road itself. If the drains discharge into a nearby river and the level of the river rises, river water may flow back through the drains, forcing the rainwater ahead of it, and sending water up through the grilles and onto the streets.

Scientists use measurements of rainfall, the type of surface, the height of the water table, and other relevant information to calculate "flood peak formulae": numbers used to predict the maximum rate at which water is likely to drain from an area. In cities, this number is much higher than it is in rural areas. In Chicago, for example, the peak flow is up to 4 times greater in the commercial and industrial areas than in residential areas, where water can drain through natural soil; this difference is typical. The measurements and calculations show that flooding is a greater risk in a city than in the countryside surrounding it, and the water rises faster, often much faster.

Cities continue below ground level. Buildings have basements and cellars, and beneath them there are service tunnels of all kinds, carrying telephone and electric cables and gas and water pipes. These flood first. Floodwater is not clean. Apart from the harm caused by soaking, a flood leaves behind a thick deposit of mud, picked up from the land over which it has swept, along with debris of all kinds. In the 1966 flood in Florence (see page 1), the river Arno shifted 1 million tons (1.1 million tonnes) of soil, rubble, furniture, and other debris. It took four weeks to clear it all, using heavy earth-moving equipment.

Floods also hamper rescue efforts. Overflowing rivers sweep away bridges. Water rushing through and beneath a town can lift sections of road and rail track and smash them, leaving them broken and piled high with rubble. Underground flooding breaks gas and water pipes and telephone and electric cables, shutting down these essential services and creating a risk of fire from gas leaks and live wires. Poles carrying overhead power and telephone lines are swept away even more easily than trees. Communities can be left isolated, with road and rail links broken and telephone lines down. A region around Omegna, near Lake Maggiore in northern Italy, was briefly isolated in this way by a flood and landslide in July 1996.

When water moves, it exerts considerable force (see box on page 14). This is sufficient to shift many loose objects, but water also has another effect. It reduces the weight of objects, making them easier to move. This is why some objects float.

This principle was discovered by the Greek mathematician and engineer Archimedes (c. 287–c. 212 B.C.). The story goes that Hieron, the king of Syracuse, where Archimedes lived, asked Archimedes to discover whether a new crown the goldsmith had just delivered was pure gold or a mixture of gold and silver—without damaging the crown. Archimedes had no idea how this might be done, until one day when his bath was a little too full, he stepped into it and some water overflowed. He realized that the volume of the water which overflowed was exactly equal to the volume of the part of his body that had entered it. This showed him how to check the crown. He was so excited that he jumped from the bath and ran naked through the streets to the palace shouting, "Eureka! Eureka!" ("I've found it!"). Silver is less dense than gold, so weight for weight it is bulkier. If Archimedes immersed the crown in water, measured the amount of water it displaced, and compared this with the volume of water displaced by the same weight of pure gold, he could tell whether the crown contained silver. It did, and the goldsmith was executed.

No one knows whether the famous tale is true, but the principle of buoyancy certainly is; you can easily demonstrate for yourself that when an object is immersed in water, it displaces a volume of water weighing as much as itself. Experiment 29 in volume 6 explains how to do this. Buoyancy is the upward force water (or any other fluid) exerts on a body immersed in it. A cubic foot (0.03 cubic meter) of water weighs 62.4 pounds (28 kilograms). If 1 cubic foot (0.03 cubic meter) of the immersed object weighs 62.4 pounds (28 kilograms) or less, it will not sink. If it weighs exactly 62.4 pounds (28 kilograms) it will have neutral buoyancy, and remain at the same level in the water. If it weighs less than this, it will bob to the surface and float. If it weighs more than 62.4 pounds per cubic foot (28 kilograms per 0.03 cubic meter), that is how much its weight will be reduced, but it will still be heavy enough to sink.

Wood floats, because it is less dense than water; 1 cubic foot (0.03 cubic meter) of oak, for example, weighs about 44 pounds (19.8 grams). Moving water, therefore, lifts wooden objects as well as pushing them forward. Metals are heavier than water, of course, and they sink. Whole objects made from metal may also contain air, however; what matters is the density of the object as a whole, not necessarily the material from which it is made. Steel sinks in water, but ships made from steel contain air, and that is why they float.

Automobiles also contain air. Modern cars are made with tightly fitting doors and windows that make them almost watertight. Imagine you are sitting in a car when floodwater washes past it. Water splashes into the engine, which stalls, leaving you immobilized. Suppose the car is 12 feet (3.6 meters) long, 5 feet (1.5 meters) wide, and weighs 1.5 tons (1.65 tonnes). The water rises around you and soon reaches the level of the floor. As it rises higher, the water exerts a buoyancy force on the car. When the water has risen one foot (0.3 meter) above the floor level, this force will amount to about 1.8 tons (1.98 tonnes). The car will then weigh less than the water beneath it. It will float, and there will be no way you can control it. The flood will be in charge, carrying you where it will. Making an allowance for the distance between the floor of the car and the road, when the flood is 2 feet (0.6 meters) deep all but the heaviest cars will float, provided the doors are shut. Open a door and water will fill the car, adding to its weight and sinking it so it stays on the road.

About half of all people killed in flash floods in the United States die trapped in automobiles that have been carried away on the waters. Eventually the vehicle is likely to enter deeper water and, despite its tightly filling doors, it will slowly fill with water and sink.

Trailers, campers, and mobile homes are also likely to float and then be thrown against one another. When the flood also brings down rocks, trees, and other large pieces of debris, the damage is compounded as this material is hurled against vehicles. This is what happened on July 7, 1996, at a campsite in the Spanish Pyrenees.

People living in more solid houses who are indoors when the floods arrive can seek shelter on upper floors and eventually the roof. They will survive, but the contents of their homes will be ruined by the water. Even worse, floodwaters can wash away ground from around buildings, weakening the structure, and this, combined with the pressure of the moving water against the sides, can cause irreparable damage. Floods can even carry away whole houses that are not firmly fixed to solid foundations. On the afternoon of June 3, 1903, a substantial wooden house in Heppner, Oregon, was carried six blocks by a flash flood. Its bottom story was reduced to splinters and, of course, the entire house was totally wrecked. Almost one-quarter of the population of Heppner died in that flood.

When the waters start to rise, many people flee their homes. There may have been some warning of the impending flood, giving the authorities time to evacuate the areas deemed to be at risk.

The scale of evacuation is often huge. In August 1996, floods in Bangladesh caused 100,000 people to flee their homes; in the same month 80,000 evacuated their homes in Hanoi when the Red River burst through a dike 30 miles (48 kilometers) upstream and flooded the city to a depth of several feet. The following month tropical storms brought widespreads flooding to central Vietnam; 114,000 people had to leave their homes. Heavy monsoon rains can devastate vast areas. They inundated 60 villages in Assam in the summer of 1996, forcing an estimated 1.5 million people to flee. The Indian authorities had to establish 120 relief camps to accommodate them. In 1995, summer rains caused floods in three provinces of China, killing at least 1,200 people and leaving 5.6 million people marooned by the waters. That flood destroyed about 900,000 homes, and accommodations had to be found for 1.3 million people.

Advance warnings usually allow enough time for evacuation, but it has not always been so, and evacuation is possible only if enough transport is available. There may not be time for people to walk to safety. Floods, especially flash floods, which arrive very suddenly, almost always cause some deaths, but the number of fatalities is much lower now than it used to be.

On April 17, 1421, the sea broke through dikes at Dort in the Netherlands, inundated polders (see page 76), and drowned 100,000 people. Asia has suffered disasters on this scale more recently. In 1876, a cyclone from the Bay of Bengal brought torrential rain to what is now Bangladesh, at a time when rivers were already at their high monsoon levels; both the Ganges and Brahmaputra rivers overflowed. The resulting flood was one of the worst natural disasters in modern history, drowning 100,000 people in just half an hour. Similar flooding in the summer of 1996 affected nearly one-third of Bangladesh and caused nearly 120 deaths. This is still a large number, but the toll was much lower than that from the 1876 flood.

In rural areas, there are fewer homes for the floods to destroy, but when fields lie under water the crops in them are ruined. If the water is flowing fast it will carry away soil (see page 85) and, along with it, fertilizer, seeds, or growing plants. Still water is no better. It will fill all the spaces between soil particles so there is no air for

Figure 26: *In Larimer County, Colorado, a view of Big Thompson Canyon and Highway 34 inundated with water after the flood of August 1976.* (U.S. Geological Survey)

the roots, and the plants will drown. When the waters recede, what remains of the crop will lie dead beneath a thick layer of mud.

Where food supplies are already barely adequate, floods can lead to famine. Floods in the summer of 1996 destroyed about one-fifth of the North Korean rice crop and 2.5 million acres (1 million hectares) of crops in China.

The destruction of crops can lead to food shortages and, more immediately, ruin the livelihoods of many people. Nearly six million people lost their homes and crops in the 1996 floods in Bangladesh. After such a catastrophe, not only does the government face the problem of replacing the lost food, it must help all those who have been left destitute.

Since floods are caused by too much water, it may seem strange that one of the most serious hazards associated with them is water shortage. Piped water supplies fail, and sewers are overwhelmed. Sewage is removed when it flows under gravity or is pumped. An overflowing river sends water in the opposite direction under great pressure. This pushes back the contents of sewers, which can then overflow into the streets. As the flood subsides, it leaves behind large pools of water in low-lying areas on the surface and in the cellars and basements of buildings. This water contains material transported by the flood and is likely to be seriously contaminated with sewage. Disease-causing bacteria flourish in these conditions, and it is all too easy for them to infect people. Diarrhea, nausea, and vomiting, the most widespread symptoms, are unpleasant and can be dangerous, especially for young children, but the illnesses can be more serious. Cholera, dysentery, and typhoid fever are among the diseases that may follow a flood, and unless treated, they can kill. Treatment requires medicines and health workers to distribute them quickly, and the diseases can be checked only by removing the contaminated water and restoring a reliable supply of clean water. The need is urgent, because these diseases can spread rapidly to become epidemics.

We often measure the cost of any disaster in monetary terms. This is convenient and allows us to compare the severity of one disaster with that of another. Counted in this way, floods are always expensive, with damage running to hundreds of millions of dollars, and sometimes more. In 1996 alone, damage due to flooding in Russia was estimated at $140 million, in South Korea at $600 million, in Canada at $200 million, in northern Europe at $2 billion, and in China at $12 billion.

A price tag tells only part of the story, however. The damage to which the tag refers is to homes, crops growing in fields, and factories, as well as the streets, bridges, and public buildings that are central to communities. It is human lives, though, that the rising waters damage, and it is ordinary people who pay the real cost—in bereavement, lost homes and possessions, jobs lost when businesses are destroyed, livelihoods ruined when crops are inundated and fishing boats smashed and sunk. In some countries, insurance may help with the cost of repairing homes and rebuilding lives; but not everyone can afford insurance, and it cannot heal the emotional wounds left by the loss of cherished possessions or the ruination of achievements resulting from a lifetime of hard work. Money can compensate far less adequately for lost lives.

Floods and Soil Erosion

Big rivers carry vast amounts of sediment. Every year, the Tennessee River transports 11 million tons (12.1 million tonnes) of soil particles, the Missouri 176 million tons (193.6 million tonnes). This movement of soil from the land to the sea continues year in and year out, although the amount a particular river carries depends on the kind of land across which it flows. In all, the United States loses about 4 billion tons (4.4 billion tonnes) of soil a year, around half of which is deposited as sediment in lakes or in the sea just off the coast.

After very heavy rain, river levels rise and the appearance of river water changes. Rivers that were once fairly clear become opaque as they turn into raging torrents, because the quantity of soil in them increases dramatically. If, then, they overflow their banks, the floodwaters flow directly over the land, carrying even more soil downhill.

Soil consists of mineral particles, formed from rock that was split when water froze and expanded inside small cracks, then was rolled by the wind and water, and battered and ground down by friction with other particles. This process is called "weathering," and differences in the composition and structure of the original rocks produce soil particles that vary widely in size. An ounce (28 grams) of dry sand contains about 2,500 grains if the sand is very coarse, and up to 1.3 million if the sand is finer. Silt particles are much smaller: 1 ounce contains about 165 million grains. Clay has the smallest particles of all: About 2.5 trillion (one thousand thousand million) grains weigh just 1 ounce. Soil may also contain organic matter comprising plant and animal remains, along with the products of their decomposition.

Pick up a handful of soil and, unless it is very dry, its particles will stick together in small lumps. While the soil is in the ground, these lumps are more or less joined to form a soil mass. When water moves soil, it must start by detaching particles or small lumps from this main mass. This is the first stage in erosion. Once the particles or lumps are detached, the water can shift them whenever heavy rain falls onto bare ground and water flows over the surface down a slope. Gradually the soil becomes deeper at the bottom of the slope and shallower at the top until eventually all the upper soil layer may be removed from patches at the top of the field, exposing the subsoil. This may be the first time the farmer notices what has been happening.

Erosion feeds on itself. Clear water dislodges few soil particles, even when it flows quite fast. As soon as it starts carrying particles, however, its power to dislodge increases greatly. The particles themselves do the work, by slamming into attached particles and knocking them free. As the water proceeds down a slope, not only does the load of soil it carries increase, but so does the rate at which it gathers particles.

Obviously, the speed of flow is important, because the kinetic energy (energy of motion) of the particles is proportional to the square of their speed (see box on page 14), but the length of the slope is even more important, for two reasons. In the first place, the water has farther to travel down a long slope than a short one, so it has more time in which to gather soil. In the second place, a larger area of ground is exposed on a long slope than on a short one and, assuming the whole of the slope is covered by moving water, there is more water to gather and transport soil.

The larger the drainage basin (see page 12) supplying a river system, the less soil that enters the river from each acre (0.4 hectare) of land. This does not mean less soil is transported, but only that more of it is deposited in relatively low-lying areas before reaching the river. The Mississippi River discharges one million tons of sediment into the sea every day, but its drainage basin is so large that this amounts to only 290 tons (319 tonnes) a year for each square mile. Much smaller basins in the San Gabriel Mountains of California lose up to 5,000 tons (5,500 tonnes) of soil per square mile annually; when fires have destroyed the chaparral vegetation, the loss can increase to as much as 100,000 tons (110,000 tonnes).

Soil is more likely to be stripped from the land surface in regions where the climate is dry than in places where rainfall is spread evenly through the year, even though rain falling in every month adds up to a greater annual total. Where the climate is dry, weeks or months may pass without rain. During this time the soil dries out thoroughly. Drying separates soil particles, except on clay soils, which shrink and harden as they bake in the hot sunshine. Watch the cloud of dust that follows an automobile traveling along a desert road and it is obvious that the soil has turned to dust or loose sand. Few plants can grow when the soil is in this condition, so the vegetation is sparse. Scattered shrubs and clumps of tough grasses are separated by bare ground.

When the rain arrives, it usually does so as a fierce storm that dumps a huge amount of rain in a very short time. Even a very porous, sandy soil cannot absorb the water fast enough to prevent it flowing across the surface, and a fine-grained soil quickly turns to waterlogged mud. The flowing water surges over the ground, carrying soil with it and leaving behind the deep gulches, arroyos, and dry washes it carves as temporary channels. These features, common in the Great Plains and western United States, are evidence of the erosive power of torrential rain. Over most of the United States east of the Rockies, storms severe enough to be regarded as rare events account for up to 90 percent of the soil particles carried by rivers.

Even then, certain places are more vulnerable than others. In the 1930s an area to the north of Salt Lake City, Utah, suffered a series of floods that caused a great deal of damage, because the floodwaters brought with them large amounts of sand, gravel, and boulders. This material was later found to have come from particular localities, making up only 10 percent of the watershed over which the waters had flowed, where overgrazing and fires had removed most of the vegetation. Grazing was stopped, the areas were given better protection from fires, and at intervals of 25 yards (22.5 meters) trenches were dug across the slope and sown with tough grasses.

In the years since, rainstorms have continued, but there have been no more floods carrying large amounts of debris.

Water that flows across the surface in a flood is lost. Floods are caused by too much water, of course, but in deserts and regions of low rainfall, all water is valuable. If that water could have been trapped and stored, it could have irrigated crops after the storms had passed.

Although dry regions are more vulnerable, few places are immune from floods and the resulting loss of soil. The upper layers of soil contain the nutrients plants need, and their loss leaves the soil much less productive. Much of the soil removed from sloping ground is deposited at a lower level. This might make it seem that one field's loss is another's gain, but it is not so simple. After the topsoil has been stripped away, less fertile subsoil is likely to follow it and then be deposited on top of the topsoil. The topsoil that accumulates is often fairly useless for farming, because it is buried beneath less fertile subsoil and the entire mass of waterborne soil, deposited as thick mud, buries the cultivated soil and the plants already growing in it. When floods course through a town, large amounts of the soil they carry are left behind as a thick layer of dirty, useless mud.

Not all the soil transported in this way is dumped onto the land. Most of it enters rivers and is carried downstream. As the river crosses almost level ground, its waters flow more slowly. They then have less energy with which to transport solid particles, and these begin to settle on the riverbed. This raises the bed, but not by the same amount everywhere. Piles of sediment collect in particular places until they rise high enough to form bars, which interrupt the water flow. During peak flows, these bars shift this way and that, but by reducing the size of the river channel they also increase the likelihood that the river will overflow its banks. By carrying away soil, a flood upstream makes it more probable that some time later the river will flood farther downstream.

If the river is dammed, the sediment will settle in the reservoir behind the dam. Reservoirs are used to store water and to generate power; the accumulation of sediment reduces their capacity to do either. About 35 years after it was built, Washington Mills Reservoir, at Fries, Virginia, was able to hold only 17 percent of the volume of water it held originally, due to sedimentation. This was an extreme case, but most reservoirs made by damming rivers lose a significant proportion of their volume in this way.

Sediment that fails to settle on the riverbed is carried all the way to the river mouth and into the sea. The soil particles are carried in fresh water. When the fresh water starts mixing with sea water, negatively charged chlorine (Cl^-) and positively charged sodium (Na^+) ions form links between electrically charged soil particles, causing them to stick together in clumps, which settle to the bottom. There the sediment can form bars across the river mouth, obstructing the navigation channel used by ships entering the river, or raise the beds of harbors so the sediment must be removed by dredging to maintain the required depth of water.

Accumulating sediment also alters the shape and location of large deltas. In some places the Mississippi delta is growing, extending the area of land into the sea, but where it is exposed to storms the adjacent coast is receding. The entire delta is also, very slowly, moving south.

Besides destroying property and crops, floods damage the land over which they flow and the rivers, reservoirs, and coasts where they deposit their loads of soil. As the example from Utah shows, however, where the dangers are clearly identified steps can be taken to reduce or eliminate them. Floods cannot be avoided altogether, but they need not be as destructive as many of them are.

Floods of the Past

Major floods always cause huge destruction and cost many lives. Even today, floods cause about 40 percent of all the property damage attributed to climatic disasters such as hurricanes, tornadoes, blizzards, and droughts. Floods are so destructive that people remember them for a long time. We have many very old myths and legends about floods, some of them referring to events that may have happened long before people began recording events in writing.

Around 9,000 years ago, at the end of the last ice age, as the glaciers retreated and the weather grew warmer, many people lived near coasts. The shore was a good place to be, because gathering nutritious shellfish was a lot easier than hunting animals. Drinkable water was available from small streams flowing off the land, and edible plants could be found within a short distance inland. Unfortunately, the melting of the glaciers was causing a rise in sea level. This did not happen gently, at the same rate everywhere. Suppose you lived a few hundred yards from the shore, at or even a little below sea level, but protected by high ground between you and the shore. As the sea level rose, gradually high tides would reach farther up the shore, and so would waves. Then there would be an unusually ferocious storm, following several days of onshore winds that pushed water against the coast. It would take only one huge storm wave coinciding with a high spring tide (see page 62) to knock a passage through the high ground and allow the sea to flow inland. Your camp would be inundated in a matter of minutes, and it might well happen at night. Floods like this must have occurred many times in many places. The few survivors from each disaster would have found their way to other communities and told their story, and no doubt the story improved with each telling.

In Asia, at about the time the sea level was rising due to the melting of ice sheets and glaciers, there may also have been a period during which the monsoons were much heavier than they are now. These monsoons would have caused the frequent and widespread flooding that gave rise to still more flood memories, in this case associated with rain rather than the rising sea.

There are many such stories, some of which may be older versions of the flood described in Genesis. The Sumerians, living at the northern end of the Persian Gulf about 5,000 years ago, believed the gods decided to send a flood to destroy all the people, but a king, Ziusudra, was warned in advance and escaped death by riding out the flood in a boat. The Babylonians, farther north, elaborated on this story. Their hero, King Atrahasis of Shurruppak, loaded his ship with his family, their goods, and birds and other animals, both wild and domesticated. The Assyrians told a similar story in which the hero, Utnapishtim, took workmen in his boat, as well as all his relatives and many animals. This story was eventually recorded in Genesis, as the flood of Noah.

In 1929, archaeologists excavating the site of the ancient city of Ur, in what is now Iraq, came across a layer of flood deposits 8 feet (2.4 meters) thick. This was clear evidence of a major flood, caused when the Euphrates River overflowed; the archaeologists dated the event to about 3200 B.C. There are also traces of floods that occurred between about 4000 B.C. and 2400 B.C. from the sites of Kish and Nineveh as well as Ur. Although Iraq now has a very dry climate, that is where many of our flood stories originated. There was never a single flood that inundated the entire planet, but smaller floods, affecting areas so large it seemed to the people experiencing them that the whole world was flooded, happened repeatedly, especially in the lands between the Euphrates and Tigris rivers. These floods may well have influenced the way society developed (see page 31).

The old stories record memories of distant events, but they also provide warnings. They tell us to beware of living on low ground near coasts and on the floodplains of large rivers, where floods are most likely. It was flooding due to a storm surge, for example, that in 1099 caused 100,000 deaths along the coasts of southern England and the Netherlands, and that killed 2,000 people in England, Belgium, and the Netherlands in 1953. On April 17, 1421, it was the sea breaking through dikes at Dort, in the Netherlands, that flooded polders (see page 76) and drowned 100,000 people.

Many large rivers periodically overflow their banks. This kind of flooding is not confined to any particular region of the world. Just such a flood once devastated the city of Timbuktu. Throughout its history, Timbuktu has been an important trading center, but it is not a place where floods seem very likely. It is in Mali, an African country bigger than Egypt that is partly in the Sahara; Mali's annual rainfall averages no more than 9 inches (22.9 centimeters). Timbuktu lies near a bend in the river Niger, to which it is linked by canals that supply its water. The Niger flooded in December 1591 because of very heavy rain near its source in Guinea; the population, then of about 40,000, was forced to flee. Floods in Tunisia, in October 1969, killed more than 300 people and left 150,000 homeless. Tunisia suffered again in the spring of 1973. On that occasion the floods destroyed about 6,000 homes, and 90 people died. In 1996, Khartoum, Sudan, was flooded following two hours of rain, and thousands of homes were destroyed.

Sometimes it is not even a river that overflows, but dry creeks and ravines. This is what happened when severe thunderstorms caused a flash flood at Farahzad, Iran, on August 17, 1954. A wall of water 90 feet high (27.4 meters) crashed without warning through a shrine where 3,000 people were worshipping. One man saw what was about to happen and shouted a warning, but more than 1,000 people died.

Australia also has a generally dry climate, but in 1955 nearly 40,000 people were made homeless when the Castlereagh, Namoi, and Gwydir rivers overflowed in New South Wales. This was but a prelude to much more severe flooding the following year, when overflowing rivers created a temporary inland sea, 40 miles (64 kilometers) wide, between the towns of Hay and Balranald.

A year later, almost to the day, one quarter of all the buildings in Putnam, Connecticut, was destroyed by the Quinebaug River. During the day and night of August 18 almost 8 inches (20.3 centimeters) of rain fell on land drained by the river, which was already saturated by rain that had fallen earlier. On the morning of August 19 a series of upstream dams failed, sending floodwater through the town (see page 53). Fortunately, everyone in Putnam survived the flood.

South Dakota was not so fortunate in June 1972. Rains in the Black Hills caused widespread flooding, and hundreds of people were killed.

The Arno River, in Italy, has flooded repeatedly. It drowned 300 people in 1333, but its most seriously damaging flood happened in November 1966 (see page 1). This is when it flooded Florence, in places to a depth of 20 feet (6 meters), and destroyed or damaged buildings of major historical importance and countless works of art.

Not all river floods are natural events. In China, they have been used as a weapon. For several centuries, as the power of the Chou dynasty declined, warlords fought one another for power and land. This period ended in 222 B.C. with the victory of one faction and the establishment of the Ch'in dynasty, but while it lasted canals, reservoirs, and dikes were built along the Yellow River and other rivers to improve the productivity of the land from which the warlords derived their wealth. It must have seemed obvious, therefore, to order the breaking of the dikes to flood the land of an enemy. Much later, in A.D. 923, a general called Tuan Ning revived the custom during a war between forces of the Liang and T'ang dynasties and flooded 1,000 square miles (2,600 square kilometers). In 1642, the leader of a peasant revolt, Li Tzu-cheng, ordered the breaking of Yellow River dikes to flood the city of Kaifeng, which he was besieging, and killed about 900,000 people. This devastating use of the Yellow River as a weapon occurred again in 1938, when Kuomintang troops broke dikes to halt a Japanese advance, flooding about 9,000 square miles (23,400 square kilometers) and killing some 500,000 Chinese civilians.

Most Yellow River floods are natural catastrophes, of course, and sometimes their scale is immense. In September and October 1887, the failure of a dike near Chengchou sent floodwater from the river coursing through 1,500 or more towns and villages and covered 10,000 square miles (26,000 square kilometers). No one really knows how many lives were lost. Estimates range from 900,000 to 2.5 million. The flood that lasted from July through November 1931 was even bigger. It covered about 34,000 square miles (88,400 square kilometers) and destroyed the homes of 80 million people. Approximately one million people drowned or died in the famine and disease epidemics that followed the flood.

China suffered twice in 1931, because the Yangtze River rose 97 feet (29.1 meters) after heavy rain and flooded. That flood, too, was followed by famine, and more than 3.7 million people died by drowning or from starvation. Famine was the cause of most of the 30,000 deaths that followed another Yangtze flood in 1954.

Southern China lies in that part of the world which experiences the summer monsoon, when the rains are concentrated in a short season of torrential downpours. A monsoon that brings more rain than usual can cause severe floods. In August 1973, for example, monsoon floods caused rivers flowing south from the Himalayas to inundate thousands of square miles of farmland in Pakistan, Bangladesh, and three Indian states. Entire towns were under water. Thousands of people died, and millions were left homeless.

At the same time as the Asian flood occurred, 200 people died in floods in Iripuato, Mexico; in October 1973 heavy rain caused flash floods in the United States, affecting a region extending from Nebraska to Texas.

America's greatest river, the Mississippi, has sometimes turned into something more closely resembling an inland sea. In August 1926, heavy rain increased the flow in the river, which went on rising until it finally overflowed its banks in April of the following year. The river level was so high that water was forced back into several tributaries, causing them to flood as well. Eventually the water covered more than 25,000 square miles (65,000 square kilometers) in seven states; the worst affected were Louisiana, Arkansas, and Mississippi. In some places the waters were 80 miles (128 kilometers) wide and 18 feet (5.4 meters) deep; it was July 1927 before they receded.

The Mississippi flooded again in January 1937, after heavy rains had caused the Ohio to flood and discharge a huge volume of water into the main river. At Cairo, Illinois, the Mississippi rose 63 feet (18.9 meters) above its usual level, and 12,500 square miles (32,500 square kilometers) were inundated, destroying 13,000 homes and causing damage costing about $418 million. In April 1973, the river and its tributaries inundated nearly 1,000 square miles (2,600 square kilometers) around the junction of the Mississippi and Missouri, at St Louis.

Ice can also cause rivers to overflow. As the spring thaw begins and the ice starts to break, loose blocks of ice are carried downstream just as the meltwater pouring into the river increases its flow. If the ice blocks become trapped, they will form a dam. This happened in 1824 in the Neva River, which flows through St. Petersburg, killing 10,000 people there and in Kronshtadt, on an island in the Neva delta.

Britain, with its mild, wet maritime climate, has suffered many floods. The Spey and Findhorn rivers in Morayshire, Scotland, flooded in August 1829; in September 1852 the Severn in central England flooded such a large area that its valley became a continuous freshwater sea. Flooding occurred in England again in the following year, and in November 1875 large parts of central London were inundated when the Thames rose, according to some accounts by more than 28 feet (8.4 meters). The worst English flood of modern times occurred in 1952, when the coastal village of Lynmouth was severely damaged in a flash flood (see page 48).

In 1963 the worst European flood disaster of modern times struck in the mountains of northeastern Italy, north of Venice and Padua. There, at the point where the Vaiont and Piave rivers join, a dam 860 feet (258 meters) high had been built to generate electric power. Completed in 1960, the dam was so well designed that it needed to be only 74 feet (22.2 meters) thick at its base. In the shape of an arch, the dam was inherently strong and, despite the tragedy that followed, it did not fail. Behind the dam, the reservoir was designed to hold about 3 billion tons (3.3 billion tonnes) of water, but by 1963 the demand for power had increased, and the water level in the reservoir was allowed to rise until it was 76 feet (22.8 meters) below the spillway at the top.

Overlooking the reservoir is the northern slope of Mount Toc, about 1 square mile (2.6 square kilometers) of which was covered by loose rock, mainly limestone, and a clay containing the remains of seashells, called marl. Although the slope was unstable, it was shallow near the base; engineers believed rock slides from the steeper upper slope would be halted lower down, before the rock reached the water. As the reservoir filled, the entire rock mass began to creep down the slope, eventually at more than half an inch a day, but engineers still believed it would stabilize itself. In April 1963, however, heavy rains brought the water level to within about 40 feet (12 meters) of the top of the dam wall. The loose rock started sliding faster, and the water level was quickly reduced. This proved difficult, because the heavy rains continued. The rain also saturated the surrounding land, raising the water table until it was very close to the surface and exerting an upward pressure on rocks on the lower slope. By the beginning of October it was evident that the rock mass was on the move, and that it covered a much bigger area than the engineers had supposed. On October 8, two outlet tunnels were opened to release water from the reservoir rapidly.

It was too late. At 10:41 P.M. on October 9, more than 314 million cubic yards (240 million cubic meters) of rock, moving at up to 70 MPH (112 KPH), fell into the reservoir. The "splash" sent waves high up the sides of the valley; one, rising 330 feet (99 meters) higher than the top of the dam, overflowed the crest of the dam. By the time the water reached the town of Longarone, 1 mile (1.6 kilometers) downstream from the dam, it was advancing as a wave 230 feet (69 meters) high. Nearly all the inhabitants of Longarone died. The wave swept on down the valley, flooding the villages of Pirago, Villanova, and Rivalta. The entire disaster lasted only 15 minutes, but killed 2,600 people.

Every year brings more floods. More crops and homes are destroyed, and more people die. The stories on which ancient legends are built are repeated endlessly. No doubt they will continue, but at least we may hope that in years to come, floods will cause less damage and fewer deaths. Engineers and scientists now understand much better why floods happen and how they may be controlled, and meteorologists are better able to predict the weather conditions likely to cause floods.

Prevention, warning, and survival

Land Drainage

If a flood occurs because water accumulates on what is ordinarily dry land, an obvious way to forestall it is to remove the water harmlessly before it can flow over the surface. This is the purpose of drainage. Since flowing water removes soil, drainage can also help reduce soil erosion and, through that, the transport of soil into rivers.

Traditionally, farmers dug ditches to drain their fields; you will still find many ditches in the countryside. Ditches prevent water from entering a field, so they are made along the top of a field at right angles to the slope. Water draining from the field above flows into the ditch, then along it and eventually into a river or lake. How much water the ditch collects depends on its depth. The deeper the ditch, the more water it will gather. Water will accumulate naturally at the bottom of a slope, perhaps waterlogging the ground and making it useless for farming. A series of ditches at intervals down a slope is very effective at preventing this.

Ditches need maintenance, however, and nowadays this is expensive and time-consuming. Unless vegetation is cleared periodically, it will choke and eventually clog the ditch. Soil, washed in from the field above, will gradually make the ditch shallower, so it collects less water, and its sides may erode. Left to itself, in time the ditch will become useless. In areas where farming is very intensive and farmland is valuable, ditches also prevent land from being cultivated, and they may interfere with the operation of farm machinery. This persuades some farmers to fill in their ditches and seek other ways of controlling the movement of water.

In some cases it is possible to replace ditches with pipes into which water is allowed to flow. These perform the same function as ditches, but once installed they are much cheaper and easier to maintain. Only the smaller ditches can be replaced by pipes, however; main ditches, into which smaller ditches feed, carry so much water that it would be prohibitively expensive to substitute pipes. Ditches may also store water, holding it until the tide or river level has fallen before discharging it, a task that would be much more difficult with a system of piping. Large ditches are often bordered by plants typical of riverbanks. This can make them valuable areas of wildlife habitat, which should be preserved wherever possible.

Vegetation itself contributes to flood protection. All plants shift water from the ground into the air (see page 27), and those which commonly grow along riverbanks are especially efficient at the task. Indeed, they are often planted in the course of land reclamation projects precisely for this reason. Plants help dry out the land and eventually, when the water table has fallen, they die and are replaced by other species.

Vegetation, most commonly grasses, can also be used to reclaim eroded gullies. When water flows across the surface, its speed is proportional to the slope and roughness of the ground. The rougher the ground, the more the flow is slowed. Grasses planted in gullies slow the flow of water, by making the surface rougher. This reduces the energy of the flow, causing soil particles to be precipitated as sediment. Gradually the gullies, turned into "green rivers," fill with soil carried from the ground to either side and trapped by the grass.

Inside a field, drains buried below ground, feeding into ditches or larger pipes, are used to lower the water table. Again, this is not a new idea. In the past, farmers wishing to drain a field in this way would dig a series of narrow trenches parallel to one another and to the slope, line them with gravel or larger stones, cover this with branches from shrubs and small trees laid along each trench, then return the soil they had removed, burying the drains. In time, of course, the plant material would decay and soil would fall in, filling the drains, so they would have to be dug all over again.

Obviously, since the drains must carry water down the slope, they must be inclined. On a hillside this is no problem, because if the drains are laid at a constant depth below the surface they will inevitably follow the natural slope of the hill. On shallower slopes, they may need to exceed the hill's slope and should have an incline no less than about 1:1000. Equally obviously, to be effective they must be able to carry as much water as is likely to drain during the heaviest rain storm.

Sandy soils, composed of relatively large particles with ample space between them (see page 8), drain well and need no help. In the heavier soils, especially clay, particles are so small and packed together so tightly that water has difficulty soaking down from the surface. The soil just below the depth reached by plowing tends to be almost waterlogged in wet weather and to bake hard in dry weather, in both cases encouraging the upper soil to waterlog, allowing rainwater to flow across the surface rather than soak into it. The cheapest way for a farmer to deal with this situation is to install "mole" drains, using a "mole plow." A mole plow does not cut a furrow like an ordinary plow. Instead, it has a vertical blade with a cylinder, shaped like a bullet, mounted horizontally at the

Figure 27: *Effect of mole drainage.*

bottom. As this device is pulled through the soil, it cuts a narrow slit with a tunnel at the bottom. Figure 27 illustrates this in cross-section. Depending on the soil, the drains are cut at intervals of about 9 feet (2.7 meters) and to a depth of 2–3 feet (60–90 centimeters), which is deep enough to penetrate the subsoil.

As figure 27 shows, as the mole plow is dragged along, it shatters the soil to either side, making fissures at an angle of about 45°. Water drains down the fissures and into the mole drain, which carries it away to a ditch or pipe. Ordinary plowing causes little disturbance, because this affects only the topmost foot or so of soil, and on a heavy clay soil a system of mole drains can last 5 or even 10 years before they start to collapse and must be cut again.

Tile drains provide a more permanent, if more expensive, way to move unwanted water and can be used in soil that is too soft for mole drains. Tile drains are made from short sections of pipe laid end to end at the bottom of a trench. Traditionally the pipes were made from porous clay. Today they are more often made from plastic and perforated with holes, because plastic pipes are cheaper and last longer. The principle is the same as that of the mole drain, but tile drains are bigger, with diameters of 6 or 7 inches (15–17 centimeters), and laid much farther apart. Again, it depends on the soil, but tile drains may be laid between 70–100 feet (21–30 meters) apart.

Field drains lower the water table by drawing water into them from either side, as shown in figure 28. The water table falls first in the region closest to the pipes, then the effect spreads to the sides; it may take several years for them to achieve their final drainage capacity. As figure 28 suggests, it is the depth of the drains rather than their spacing that determines the extent to which the water table is lowered.

Drainage improves the quality of wet farmland, which is why it is popular with farmers. It also helps prevent flooding in low-lying areas by diverting water into rivers or ponds where it can be held until river levels have fallen sufficiently for the water to be released, and by preventing soil erosion and the consequent raising of river-beds (see page 88).

The system that removes surplus water from fields is similar to that which removes surplus water from the streets, buildings, and parking lots of our towns. There the water flows through grilles and into storm drains. Like field drains, storm drains must be large enough to carry the maximum amount of water ever likely to flow into them. They must also discharge at a point lower than the area they drain. This presents difficulties in some cities, where there are areas below the level of the river that receives the discharge, and storm water must be pumped to the higher level.

Near coasts and on river floodplains, however, land drainage may increase the risk of floods (see page 45). There the only certain way to protect buildings is to locate them out of reach of the waters. Floodplains are often defined as land vulnerable to 100-year floods (see page 44). If a house is designed to last 70 years, there is a strong chance that it will be flooded at least once if it is built on a

Figure 28: *Effect of field drainage on water table.*

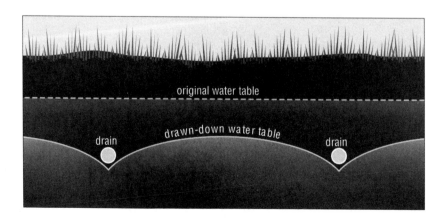

floodplain or near the coast within reach of a 100-year flood. The only way to avoid the risk is to set buildings back from the limit floodwaters are expected to reach.

Much the same policy may be best for coastal areas where erosion is a problem (see page 68) and in areas where hurricanes may cause storm surges. Some engineers who specialize in construction projects in coastal areas believe erosion and flood risks should be calculated on the basis of a 100-year probability, similar to that used on floodplains, and all buildings should be set back an appropriate distance from the shore.

Wetlands

Swamps, marshes, salt marshes, and mudflats seem dull, useless places, but often they are in locations that could be made attractive. They can be drained and turned into dry land suitable for building homes or tourist hotels. Once that is done, more people can move into what has been made a desirable area. At one time, these wetland areas occupied nearly 350,000 square miles (910,000 square kilometers) in the United States. Then, in 1849 and 1850, Congress passed the Swamp Land Acts to encourage drainage, mainly to turn what were seen as "useless" areas into farmland. Today only about 155,000 square miles (403,000 square kilometers) of wetlands remain. About 90 percent are inland, the rest along coasts where, in southernmost regions, they include mangrove swamps.

The loss of wetlands is not confined to the United States, of course. Wetlands are being lost throughout the world. As long ago as 1971 an international conference was held at Ramsar, Iran, to seek ways of protecting such areas, because they form chains of habitat for migrating water birds. The result was the Ramsar Convention on Wetlands of International Importance, under which especially valuable sites can be designated and protected from draining and development. The convention has been signed by 92 countries, and a total of 776 sites have been identified and placed on the Ramsar list. Together they cover an area of more than 200,000 square miles (520,000 square kilometers): about the area of France, or of Colorado and Wyoming combined. In the United States, the Coastal Zone Management Act of 1972 encourages states to regulate development in coastal areas generally, and an executive order issued by President Carter in 1977 made it federal policy to conserve wetlands. The Fish and Wildlife Service defines wetlands as transitional places between dry-land and aquatic areas, where saturation with water is the dominant factor determining the kind of soil and plants, and the water table is usually at or close to the surface.

Wetlands are of great importance to wildlife, but many wetlands also serve a secondary purpose. They greatly reduce the risk of flooding and can recharge aquifers (see page 46) by feeding water into them.

South of Lake Okeechobee, Florida, the Everglades is the most famous wetland area in the United States, now less than half of its original size. During the summer rainy season, the entire area used to become a slow-moving river about 80 miles (128 kilometers) wide and just a foot or two (30–60 centimeters) deep, carrying water overflowing from Lake Okeechobee down to the sea. In winter the flow ceased and the area dried into a vast meadow of a sedge called sawgrass, with clumps of trees on slightly higher ground, although no land rises more than 7 feet (2.1 meters) above sea level. The sawgrass readily caught fire, and repeated fires prevented the establishment of woody plants on the low ground. The region maintained itself and was a haven for wildlife.

Hurricanes and heavy rains caused serious flooding of adjacent land in 1926, and in 1928 a severe hurricane caused floods in which more than 1,800 people died. The U.S. Corps of Engineers and the South Florida Water Management District set to work to control the flow of water. Dikes, pumps, channels, and spillways now direct the water along prescribed routes. This increased the area available for farming, and channels linking Lake Okeechobee directly with the sea reduced the risk of flooding; the changes also prevented the seasonal floods from recharging the groundwater, leading to shortages of fresh water, and drainage from farmlands enriched the surface water with plant nutrients. Much of the area is now conserved and is being restored to something like its former condition.

There used to be similar wetland areas along the lower reaches of many big rivers, including the Mississippi. These wetland areas absorbed water overflowing from their rivers and so protected adjacent land from flooding.

Beside rivers there are often low-lying fields where the ground is usually wet. Sedges grow there, and you may see cattails, rushes, and other plants that look like grasses but are not. They grow in isolated clumps, and here and there you may find small pools of water with different plants. Part of the time some of these areas are dry enough for cattle to graze, and there may be enough grass for the farmer to be able to cut it for hay. These areas are known as "wet meadows" or, in Britain, "water meadows." Where the water lies deeper, for much more of the time, they are marshes.

From time to time, after very heavy rain or when snow melts on the hills, the water level in the river rises and may overflow the

Figure 29: *Numa Ridge bog in Glacier National Park, Montana.* (U.S. Geological Survey/P. Carrara)

banks. Then it inundates the adjacent wetland. The water may remain there until the river level falls again, then slowly drain back into the river, or water may flow across the wetland, effectively making the river that much wider, but at the same time slowing its rate of flow. Further downstream the water will drain back into the main river channel again.

Suppose the wetland is drained. During dry weather, when the river is low, drains are installed below ground (see page 95) to lower the water table by moving water into the river. Then the river bank is sealed, so water cannot seep back. Now the riverside fields can be farmed or houses can be built on them, with a fine view of the river. This kind of development has occurred many times. As the land below the houses dries, the weight of the houses depresses it and the foundations crack. At the same time, septic tanks also crack and leak their contents into the river, polluting water that people farther downstream might need for irrigation and harming aquatic plants and animals.

Then the river level rises and overflows, as it had always done periodically, but there is no longer a belt of wetland to capture and control the movement of water. Instead there are fields growing crops or homes in which people are living. The water flows into and floods them, then continues downstream unchecked, to cause flooding there as well. Land beside the river had often flooded in the past, but the flood had been limited and harmless. The plants growing beside the river thrived in the wet conditions, and land-dwelling animals moved out of the way and returned when the water subsided. Floods became harmful only after the wetland was drained and put to other uses.

Along low-lying coasts the effect is even more dramatic. There the wetlands not only absorb water as the sea rises, they also absorb the energy of waves. This reduces the likelihood of storm surges sweeping inland.

Water moves from the land into the sea, most of it through rivers, but some by draining directly from coastal lands, or through small streams. Soil particles and sand grains, suspended in the fresh water, start to settle as they meet and mix with salt water (see page 88). Sand banks and mudflats form, eventually to a height that leaves them exposed at low tide. Moving water cuts channels through them, so they come to resemble low ground with many small rivers flowing across it. Already the banks and flats are important for conservation. Mollusks burrow into them in vast numbers and provide food for wading birds.

When parts of the surface lie above the water all the time, except at spring tides and when big waves wash over them, plants can begin to grow. These trap more sediment, raising the surface still higher, and the sand bank or mudflat turns into a salt marsh, a place covered with plants that can tolerate both fresh and salt water. At low tide parts of the salt marsh are dry enough to walk on; this is what encourages developers to exploit them, although in their natural state they often provide some grazing for livestock and opportunities for raising shellfish in the channels.

Figure 30: Cross-section of a salt marsh.

The first step in reclaiming salt marshes is usually to shelter them behind a sea wall. Salt water can no longer cover them, and gradually the salt is washed from the soil, which is then very fertile.

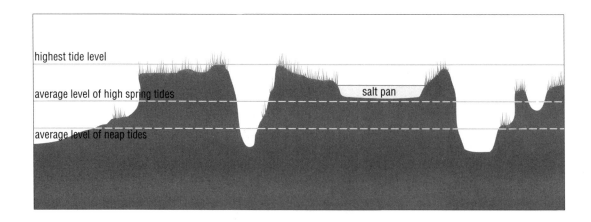

In fact, salt marshes are quite complex. As the cross-section in figure 30 shows, the high areas are intersected by channels, some extending below the average level of the low neap tides, through which water flows in both directions. Small hollows just above the average level of spring tides will catch water from waves and hold it long enough for much of the water to evaporate, increasing the salinity of the remaining water and producing a "salt pan."

Salt marshes vary in size and the range of plants they support according to local conditions. The more sheltered the coast, the bigger the salt marsh, but even on fairly exposed coasts plants may become established at the highest tide level. Waves are slowed as they pass over the sand, mud, and plants. They lose energy and strike the land behind the marsh with less force, protecting the adjacent inland area, and buildings on it. This is true even when the inland area is protected by its own sea wall, because the salt marsh protects the wall, reducing the amount of reinforcement it needs and the cost of its maintenance.

Mangrove swamps are the tropical equivalent of salt marshes. They develop best on muddy, sheltered coasts, often behind barrier islands or coral reefs. At high tide only the crowns of the trees project above water, and some of the lower leaves may be immersed most of the time. There are about 90 species of mangrove trees. All of them are broadleaved, evergreen trees or shrubs that grow poorly, if at all, away from salt water. Some have stilt roots that hold the main stem well clear of the water; others have "pneumatophores," or "breathing roots," that project above the water from the main, underground root and allow oxygen and carbon dioxide to pass into and out of the plant. Mangroves are even better at trapping sediment than are salt marsh plants. Indeed, mangroves are so good at trapping sediment that in many places they gradually extend the coastline by moving farther into the sea as the trapped sediment accumulates and the water becomes shallower.

Like the salt marshes and mudflats of temperate regions, mangrove swamps have been cleared extensively. Their wood is valuable for building and fuel, land reclaimed from them can be made into fertile farmland, especially good for growing sugarcane, and their location on sheltered coasts encourages tourist development. They have also been victims of war. During the Vietnam war mangroves were repeatedly sprayed to remove their leaves, and many died.

Wetlands, along coasts and beside rivers and lakes, absorb floodwater. They fill quickly, then release their water slowly, a little at a time as river or sea levels fall. Where they occur naturally they provide excellent flood protection. Removing them removes that protection and leaves the reclaimed land vulnerable.

Levees

When a river overflows, the water is slowed as it rises over the banks. As the water slows and loses energy, some of its load of soil particles may be deposited on top of the bank and remain there. After the flood has subsided, the sediment on the bank dries and, if it is made of clay particles, it becomes hard and solid. The bank has been raised a little, and each time the river floods, it is raised further. At the same time, sediment deposited on the riverbed may be raising its level. Ordinarily this would make the river shallower, and more prone to flooding, but the raised embankments prevent this. Instead, the entire river rises, the bed and banks building upward together, until the river may flow at a higher level than the land to either side.

Such embankments can form naturally, so it is not surprising that people living near rivers that now and then flooded their fields and homes realized long ago that they could build similar embankments to protect themselves. Embankments were built along the left bank of the Nile in the time of the pharoahs, extending for more than 600 miles (960 kilometers) from Aswân to the Mediterranean, and the right bank was protected later by Arab engineers. In Mesopotamia embankments were built along the Tigris and Euphrates, and they were also built along the great Chinese rivers. Some historians believe organizing the vast amount of labor needed for these engineering projects encouraged the development of strong community life.

Since about 1718, a raised embankment of this kind has been known as a "levee," from the French *levée*, meaning "raised," but it was in America, not France, that it was given this name. What is now Louisiana was then a French colony, and in 1718 the sieur de Bienville, its governor, decided that a town should be built on the east bank of the Mississippi at a point where there was access to several important waterways, in addition to the river itself. The town was named La Nouvelle Orléans in honor of the regent, the duc d'Orléans.

Although the chosen site was on relatively high ground, there was clearly a risk of flooding from the huge river, and a levee was built to protect it. At first the levee was quite small, but it was extended as the city grew, and by 1735 levees extended 30 miles (48 kilometers) upstream of New Orleans and 12 miles (19.2 kilometers) downstream, although they were only about 3 feet (90 centimeters) high. The levees were earth embankments, nearly 20 feet (6 meters) wide at the top, and more were built as farmers settled along the river.

Then a difficulty arose. Landowners built their own levees to protect their property, but this left gaps, and not all the levees were well maintained. The same difficulty arose in ancient China and everywhere else that embankments have been used to prevent flooding. If floodwater can flow through or over a levee in only one place, it will inundate the land downstream, regardless of how big and robust the other banks may be. The need to supervise and enforce the building and maintenance of the levees led to a more organized community life, just as it has done wherever people have relied on them. By the 1830s levee districts had been established along the Mississippi, and inspectors with powers of enforcement made regular examinations.

The U.S. Army Corps of Engineers built some Mississippi embankments. At first this was in order to improve navigation, but severe flooding in 1849 and again in 1850 persuaded Congress to release funds for the Corps of Engineers to build levees for flood protection. Levees continued to be built, higher as well as longer, until by the 1960s there were more than 3,500 miles (5,600 kilometers) of them along the Mississippi, with an average height of 24 feet (7.2 meters).

Other major rivers were also bordered by levees, but the cost was high and the protection far from complete. Embankments were constantly under attack from erosion and also from animals that burrowed into and weakened them. Thousands of people had to be permanently employed repairing them, yet they were breached repeatedly. Water would leak through holes, often animal burrows, and other weak points, bubbling through the other side in what were called "boils." These were often the cause of breaks in embankments, called "crevasses." All the same, despite the difficulties, levees do afford quite good protection and have prevented much flooding. It is only in this century, as scientists have learned more about the way river water flows, that levees have been only one of several methods employed, thus achieving better protection.

Originally, the idea was that the speed of the water in a river was the only factor determining the amount of sediment the river carried. If the river was confined within reinforced banks or levees, it was believed that when the river had to carry more water, it would flow faster and cut a deeper channel for itself. This is generally true, and large amounts of water are sometimes released into dammed rivers to clear excess sediment from them (see page 114), but all rivers are not the same. In some, a faster flow may erode the banks rather than deepening the channel. In others, including parts of the lower Mississippi, sediment that would once have been deposited on land inundated by floods is carried farther downstream and deposited on the riverbed there, making the river shallower. This kind of sedimentation contributed to six major floods between 1881 and 1890. Where levees confine a river securely, at times of peak flow they make the water level rise higher than it would if the river had been able to overflow its banks, and the embankments must be built higher to compensate. Although levees protect against flooding, they can also contribute to their own erosion and failure and increase the risk of flooding downstream.

Luck also plays a part. During the catastrophic Mississippi flood of 1927, when more than 25,000 square miles (65,000 square kilometers) were inundated, the levees were breached in many places, but the circumstances were unusual. Eastern tributaries of the main river usually carry their maximum flow in late winter and spring, from January through April. The Missouri and its tributaries, entering from the west, carry their peak flow in June. This allows the Mississippi to carry first one peak flow and then, after an interval, the other. In 1927, however, the peaks happened at the same time in all the tributaries, and the Mississippi and its levees were overwhelmed. Ten years later, in January and February 1937, the Ohio overflowed to cause the biggest flood in its recorded history, and at Cairo, Illinois, the Mississippi rose 63 feet (18.9 meters) above its usual level. Water flowed back into the smaller tributaries, which were not protected by levees, but in the lower Mississippi itself the embankments held, even while 2 million cubic feet of water were flowing along it every second. In fact, since 1928 there have been no serious crevasses in levees in the lower Mississippi valley.

Levee protection is now augmented in other ways. Setting embankments farther back from the riverbank allows some land to flood harmlessly and reduces wear on the levees themselves. Above Baton Rouge, for example, the distance between levees is less than a mile in some places and in others as much as 15 miles (24 kilometers).

Probably the most effective way of preventing floods is to remove the water before it can overwhelm the river system. Channels, controlled by floodgates, can be cut from the river to a natural depression in the land, as illustrated in figure 31. At times of peak flow, when flooding is likely, opening the floodgates diverts some of the water into the depression, from where it can be returned to the river when the flood risk has passed.

Obviously, this method is not possible everywhere. There may be no depression that is large and deep enough to be useful, or there may be houses in the only suitable depression. Where water diversion can be used, however, it usually succeeds. The Tigris and Euphrates are prevented in this way from flooding Baghdad and the farmland around it. The Euphrates is linked to Lake Habbaniyah, and a channel 41 miles (65.6 kilometers) long links the Tigris with the Tatar depression. Dams are often used to hold back peak flows in much the same way (see page 108).

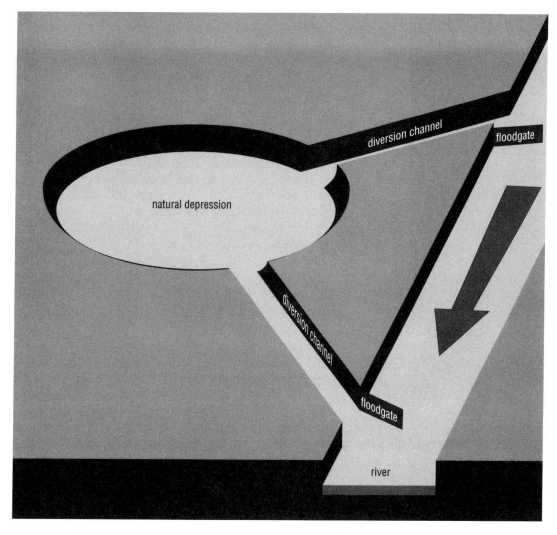

It is sometimes possible to help the river itself by increasing its carrying capacity. The rate at which river water flows is determined by the cross-sectional area of its channel and its angle of slope. Widening and deepening channels has some effect, but rivers can also be made steeper. Suppose, during part of its course, the height of the riverbed falls from 100 feet (30 meters) to 50 feet (15 meters) above sea level, but the river meanders, so its length over that part of its course is 20 miles (32 kilometers). This is a fall of 1 foot (30 centimeters) in every 2,112 feet (633.6 kilometers). Join some of the meanders together with channels, however, and the water will not have so far to travel. Suppose these channels halve the distance, from 20 miles (32 kilometers) to 10 miles (16 kilometers). This doubles the gradient to 1 foot (30 centimeters) in every 1,056 feet (316.8 kilometers), so the water will flow faster. If the water flows

Figure 31: *Flood prevention by diverting river flow.*

faster, more of it can be discharged from the river each second, which can be enough to prevent flooding. Where the river is meandering, the channels are usually cut as broad curves, to reduce erosion that can form new meanders, but when low-lying land is reclaimed from the sea, straight channels are often satisfactory. Channels for this purpose were constructed along the Mississippi in the 1930s. A total of 16 channels reduced the length of the river between Memphis, Tennessee, and Baton Rouge, Louisiana, by 170 miles (274 kilometers).

Whether they are called levees, dikes, or embankments, walls to raise the height of riverbanks have been used to prevent flooding for thousands of years. They have been discovered independently in many parts of the world and, by and large, they have succeeded. Today, engineers know more about the way rivers carry water and can compensate for the deficiencies of levees. Using alternative methods in conjunction with levees, even the biggest rivers can be tamed most of the time.

Dams

Almost since prehistoric times, people have built dams to control the flow of rivers. The remains have been found of a dam built by the ancient Egyptians in about 4000 B.C., the Mesopotamians built them, and the Romans built many. Dams were built for several reasons. Some were used to store water for irrigation or domestic use during the dry season. Others held back water during times of high river flow and released it gradually during times of low flow. This regulated the flow of the river, so the amount of water downstream of the dam remained constant at all times. Dams were used to collect sediment in order to prevent the silting up of harbors, and to form artificial lakes for the use of ships transporting cargoes.

When the first factories were built to concentrate manufacturing in particular places using large machines, steam power had not yet been invented. At first the machines were driven by water power, provided by waterwheels. These required a reliable supply of flowing water, and more dams were built to produce it. As steam replaced water power, those dams were no longer needed, but more recently the technology of the waterwheel has been adapted to make turbines, used to generate electrical power. This has led to the building of still more dams. Today, more than one-fifth of all the world's electricity is generated by water flowing through dams.

Many modern dams are very large. In the world as a whole, there are more than 60,000 dams over 50 feet (15 meters) high, with reservoirs behind them holding more than 1,400 cubic miles (5,740 cubic kilometers) of water. Some dams are much higher than 50 feet. Nowadays a large dam is defined as one that is more than 492

Figure 32: *Construction of Richard B. Russell Dam and Power Plant, Savannah, Georgia.* (U.S. Army Corps of Engineers)

feet (147.6 meters) high, or has a volume of more than 196 million cubic yards (149.8 million cubic meters), or has a reservoir holding enough water (about 6.25 billion U.S. gallons, or 23.75 billion liters) to cover 12 million acres (4.8 million hectares) to a depth of 1 foot (30 centimeters). The Aswân High Dam is 364 feet (109.2 meters) high and 2.3 miles (4.4 kilometers) long (see page 35). Few dams are as long as the Aswân, although the Chapeton Dam will be almost 140 miles (224 kilometers) long and the Pati Dam 109 miles (174.4 kilometers) long, when these are completed. Both are on the Paraná River in Argentina. By modern standards, however, the Aswân Dam is not especially high. The first large dam to be built was the Hoover Dam on the Colorado River. It was completed in 1936 and stands 726 feet (217.8 meters) high. The Mauvoisin Dam, on the Drance de Bagnes River, Switzerland, is 777 feet (233.1 meters) high, and the Vaiont Dam, in northern Italy, is 858 feet (257.4 meters) high (see page 93). Several others are only slightly smaller. The Aguamilpa Dam, on the Santiago River, Mexico, for example, is 613 feet (183.9 meters) high, and the Lhakwar Dam, on the Yamuna River, India, is 670 feet (201 meters) high.

Size is only one measure of a dam and is determined by the dimensions of the valley in which it is built. Many rivers are dammed repeatedly along their courses. The river is then said to be "cascaded." The Ohio, Tennessee, Missouri, upper Mississippi, and Columbia are among the American rivers that have been cascaded. The Columbia, in Washington state, has the longest cascade; its series of 12 dams begins near the Canadian border and ends at the coast, about 640 miles (1,024 kilometers) away. The cascade begins with the Grand Coulee Dam, 550 feet (165 meters) high and more than ¾ mile long, which is the most important member of the cascade in controlling river flow and preventing floods.

Most early dams were made from earth, rock, or some combination of the two. Building even a small dam is a major undertaking and uses a huge amount of material, so it was natural to use earth and rock, which were available locally. The first dams were probably made entirely from clay or other fine-grained soil that would be fairly impermeable when packed tightly. A dam of this kind, made from a single material, is described as "homogeneous."

A cubic foot of water weighs 62.4 pounds, so even a small reservoir exerts considerable pressure against a dam. This means the dam wall must be substantial and usually much thicker at its base than at the top, so in vertical cross-section the wall is triangular. The slope of the wall must be sufficient to prevent the earth or rock from slumping to the bottom. It must also distribute the weight of the wall, to prevent the ground beneath it from being depressed and causing the dam to collapse. On the upstream side the wall must resist the action of waves, and on the downstream side it must resist erosion by rain. Vegetation can be planted on the downstream side to bind the earth together. Rocks of varying sizes, called "riprap," can be piled against the upstream face to absorb the energy of waves. Alternatively, the upstream face can be protected by a surface of masonry, concrete, or asphalt.

Earth and rock are still widely used, but nowadays many dam walls also contain steel, concrete, and solid masonry. There are five basic types of construction, shown in figure 33, in each case with the reservoir to the left. The one to be used is chosen for its appropriateness to the site, and a cascade often includes dams of several types. In all the drawings in figure 33, the steepness of the slopes has been exaggerated to save space. In real dams, the base is much wider than it is shown here.

An earth dam may be homogeneous, but more commonly it has a core of impermeable clay with an outer layer of compacted earth, with a rock (riprap) cladding protecting its upstream face. Earth dams can be built on soft ground, because they are so wide at the base that their weight is distributed over a large area. Rockfill dams are more substantial, but they are also heavier and need a solid foundation. As the name suggests, they are made from loose rocks of varying sizes, and the upstream face is protected by solid

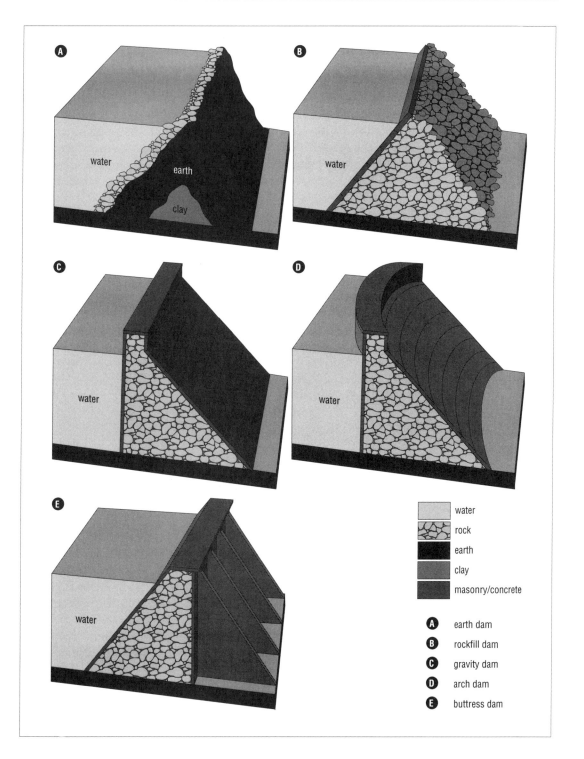

Figure 33: *Dam types.*

masonry, concrete, or asphalt. The facing must be impermeable to prevent water penetrating the structure.

Earth and rockfill dams slope on both the upstream and downstream sides, but a gravity dam has a vertical face on the upstream side. It is made from rocks or concrete blocks held together with cement and faced with concrete. A gravity dam is extremely heavy; its weight secures it to the foundation. It is held in place by gravity, hence the name. The weight of a gravity dam is spread by the wide base. Although the design looks modern, the first gravity dams were built in Spain in the 16th century, and two of them are still in use. The arch dam is a variant of the gravity dam. Its great weight secures it. The arch dam curves upstream; this shape transmits the water pressure to the sides, pushing the dam into the banks and increasing its strength. The Hoover Dam is of this type, but some arch dams have more than one arch. The Bartlett Dam, on the Verde River, Arizona, is 800 feet (240 meters) long and has 10 arches. It is the upstream face of a buttress dam that slopes, often at about 45°, and the downstream face that is vertical, but on the downstream side the dam is supported by buttresses.

Once a river has been blocked by a dam, water will accumulate behind the dam to form an artificial lake. Eventually, the water level in the lake will reach the top of the basin containing it. Dams are never as high as the valleys containing them, so water cannot spill over the sides of the lake onto the surrounding countryside, but unless water is also allowed to flow through or past the dam, at times it will overflow it. In the case of an earth dam, this will wash away the top of the structure and after a time destroy the dam. If the base of the dam is weak, water may flow through it and escape that way, washing away the wall until the dam collapses. Even dams made from solid masonry or concrete must allow excess water to escape in a controlled fashion. All dams, therefore, have either spillways in the center or on one or both sides, or pipes at the base through which water can be discharged, or some combination of both. Regulating the outflow of water through the dam allows the water level behind the dam to be kept low enough below the crest to prevent waves washing over the top. The distance between the crest and the maximum height the water is allowed to reach is called the "freeboard." If a dam is to be used for power generation, pipes carry water through the structure, allowing it to fall from a high to a low level and flow past turbines before being discharged on the downstream side.

Whatever their primary purpose, dams provide excellent flood protection. Probably the most famous of all dam-building and flood control projects was that begun in 1933 by the Tennessee Valley Authority (TVA). It was unique in that it brought together projects already being run by a number of government agencies and based them on the drainage basin of a river system. The project's aims were to control floods on the Tennessee River and its tributaries, improve navigation, and generate electrical power. It was a spectacular success at preventing serious flooding and much admired in other countries, not least for the social improvements it brought to the area under its administration. Its 18 reservoirs behind dams on the Tennessee and its tributaries hold enough water to cover 12 million acres (4.8 million hectares) to a depth of 1 foot, 30 centimeters (6.25 billion U.S. gallons, or 23.75 billion liters). In February 1957, the Tennessee would have inundated Chattanooga had the surplus water not been held in reservoirs. Instead of rising to 54 feet (16.2 meters), the river reached only a little over 32 feet (9.6 meters). A year later, in May 1958, TVA reservoirs saved Cairo, Illinois, from flooding. Six dams built along the Missouri since 1944, combined with levees (see page 104) to protect vulnerable farmland and towns, have prevented flooding, and hydroelectric plants built into the dams generate enough power to meet all the needs of Nebraska. The dams hold back 105 reservoirs spread along a chain 1,000 miles (1,600 kilometers) long, with a total capacity of 75 million acre-feet. That is more than 400 billion gallons.

This success has been repeated on many rivers, but there are risks. Should a dam fail, the result is catastrophic flooding of the valley downstream. Failures are rare, but they do happen. The Puentes Dam, a gravity dam on the Guadalentín River, Spain, completed in 1791, failed in 1802 when unusually heavy rain delivered more water to the reservoir than the dam could hold.

Another gravity dam, the St. Francis in California, was constructed on geologically unstable foundations and collapsed in 1928, two years after it was completed. Concrete dams need solid foundations, on young rock that has not been eroded and cracked by weathering. When Clover Dam, a small buttress dam, was being built on the Kiewa River, Australia, weathering beneath some of the buttresses caused seepages that were difficult to repair. A small fault beneath the foundation caused the collapse of the Malpasset Dam, an arch dam on the Reyran River in southern France, in November 1959.

In Spain, the Monte Jacques Dam, also an arch dam, had to be abandoned completely, not because of cracks but due to caverns in the surrounding limestone rock. The dam was built and its reservoir filled, but water leaked into and through the caverns. Despite attempts to seal it, it proved impossible to make the reservoir watertight, and it has never held water. The Kentucky Dam, on the Tennessee River, suffered similar problems. In this case they were cured, using hay, bitumen, and cement to seal the reservoir, but the cost was very high.

On June 5, 1976, the Teton Dam in Snake River Valley, Idaho, collapsed. This earth dam, 305 feet high and more than half a mile long, failed as its reservoir was filling and contained about 109 billion cubic feet (2.94 billion cubic meters) of water, 97 percent of its planned capacity. The resulting flood covered 25 square miles (65 square kilometers) and left 30,000 people homeless. The huge Vaiont Dam did not fail, but the overflow occurred when a mountainside collapsed into it, releasing a large volume of water and causing many deaths (see page 93).

Most major rivers experience a large seasonal variation in the amount of water they carry. A rainy season or melting snow increases the flow, and once all the snow has melted a dry season reduces it. Dams regulate the flow, so it is constant through the year, but this alters the river downstream from the dam.

Seasonal floods along the Colorado River used to deposit sand along the banks, forming beaches, but the slower, regulated flow downstream from the Glen Canyon Dam caused the sand to settle along the bed. Wildlife habitats changed, and scientists realized this was because habitats needed the periodic floods to maintain them, so they tried reinstating the spring flood. From March 26 to April 2, 1995, the dam released water as fast as it could through the Grand Canyon. When the ordinary flow resumed, 55 new beaches had appeared and 75 percent of the existing ones had grown bigger. Bankside vegetation that had grown into the slow-moving water was washed away, marshes and backwaters were revitalized, and habitats were improved for many species. The flood caused minor damage to some habitats, but overall it was judged a great success, and scientists began looking for other rivers that might benefit.

The next river to be treated was the Trinity, in Trinity County, northern California. It was dammed in 1963, and the slower flow allowed vegetation to grow out from the banks, reducing habitats for turtles, frogs, insects, and fish, and gravel beds used by salmon for spawning filled with sand. Floods lasting several days have been made each year since 1991 by releasing water rapidly from the dam. Similar treatment is being considered for other rivers. Man-made floods are controversial, especially in those parts of the West where water is in short supply, but they do help maintain natural wildlife in and beside a river while retaining the advantages of the dam.

Dams are very successful at preventing flooding, but in the past they have caused problems by damaging habitats and altering patterns of downstream sedimentation, and occasional dam failures have caused appalling calamities. Scientists and engineers now understand much more than they did even a few years ago about the way rivers transport water, about identifying suitable sites for building dams and how to build them safely, and about the wildlife habitats rivers provide and how to protect them. The risks are being reduced, but the advantages remain.

Canalization

Rivers cause flooding because they are not always big enough to carry all the water trying to flow through them. One remedy is to alter the river channel itself by rebuilding and rerouting it. Levees (see page 104) raise the banks of a river and so they are a form of river rebuilding, but the process can go much further. The river can be widened or deepened, bends can be removed, and the bed can be smoothed and leveled and its gradient increased to make water flow faster.

On a still larger scale, canals are sometimes built to link two adjacent drainage basins and move water from one to the other. One of the most ambitious proposed schemes of this kind would have redirected two Siberian rivers so instead of flowing north, they would carry water south to irrigate farmlands. That plan was abandoned, but similar projects are planned or being developed in Canada, China, Mexico, and the United States.

One of the biggest is in Sudan. At present more than half the flow in the White Nile is lost by evaporation as the river passes through the Sudd swamps in southern Sudan. When the Jonglei Canal is completed, it will be about 225 miles (360 kilometers) long and will bypass the swamps, thereby providing Sudan and Egypt with an additional 1 billion U.S. gallons (3.8 billion liters) of water a year.

Such major engineering of rivers is called "canalization" or "channelization." A canal is like a river, but one built by engineers in a place where no river flows naturally; of course, the water in it is static. That difference remains, but the more a natural river is altered by engineering, the more it comes to resemble a canal. If levees are included as a type of canalization, most of the great rivers of the world have been canalized along at least parts of their courses, and in years to come many more miles of river will be modified.

Floodwater is usually lost, but canalization can be used to redirect it to where it is needed. Channels cut from the river can convey water to farmland for irrigation.

Canalization is very effective. Provided the size and route of the channel are calculated accurately, it will divert water that would otherwise have caused flooding. Two channels, a little more than half a mile (0.8 kilometer) apart and 19 miles (30.4 kilometers) long, cross a low-lying part of eastern England and discharge their water into the sea. These channels were built two centuries ago, and the water they remove has converted nearly 50,000 acres (20,000 hectares) of marsh and swamp into very fertile farmland. In England and Wales, more than 25,000 miles (40,225 kilometers) of rivers have been canalized for flood prevention.

Unfortunately, modifying rivers in this way also has disadvantages, especially for wildlife. Many rivers in the northern hemisphere were once bordered by swamp or forest; this environment supported many native plants and animals. Today the swamps have been drained, many of the riverside trees are gone, and the habitats are poorer. Otters, for example, rest and breed in dens along riverbanks, in some places preferring to make these among the roots of large trees. Many of these trees are gone, because at high flow the river washes soil from around their roots, and eventually they fall into the water. The otters have not minded this, because there have always been more trees, but such sites are much less common now than they were.

Riverbank trees shade the water, and their leaves fall into the river. Without these trees, there is less food for aquatic animals, and water temperatures are more extreme. Leveling the riverbed also affects wildlife. In a natural river, some parts are deeper than others, providing a variety of conditions suitable for different species. Big rocks and overhanging stretches where the river has undercut its bank provide sheltered places. Engineering usually destroys these habitats, so the riverbed is the same everywhere.

Careful planning of canalization can now minimize the harm to wildlife, which is due to exerting more control on rivers than is necessary for flood prevention. Indeed, excessive canalization can cause water problems quite apart from the effect on natural habitats. It can even transfer the flood risk downstream.

When a river is canalized along a stretch where it is prone to flood, instead of overflowing, the water is made to flow much faster. At times of peak flow this can cause a rush of water from the canalized section into the unprotected channel downstream, greatly increasing the peak flow there. There are no more floods where they used to happen, but there may be floods farther downstream in places that used to be safe. The increased rate of flow may also cause severe erosion of riverbanks downstream from the canalized stretch.

It is also possible for canalization to transform an excess of water into a deficit. This happens if the more rapid flow increases the rate at which water drains from surrounding land, lowering the water table. When this occurs sliding gates, called "sluices," must be installed to control the flow into the canalized stretch.

Canalization reduces the risk of floods, but there are risks in engineering the flow of water in a river. Without careful planning, river engineering can generate serious problems.

Flood Predictions

Levees, dams, and the management of rivers and wetlands have done much to protect homes and farms from floods, but so far it has proved impossible to prevent floods altogether. Floods still happen, even if they are less frequent than they once were, and when they happen they are as destructive as ever. Although there is no way to guarantee absolute protection of property, it has been possible to greatly reduce the loss of life. Nowadays, many people escape harm because they are warned in advance that flooding is likely.

Weather monitoring and forecasting are now fairly accurate for several days ahead. Satellites observe the entire planet, sending a constant stream of pictures that allow meteorologists to watch weather systems as they develop and move. Hurricanes and typhoons can be watched, tracked, and their behavior predicted. You might think, therefore, there would be little problem in telling people living in low-lying areas near rivers or coasts to expect floods whenever unusually heavy rain is on its way. Unfortunately, it is not so simple. Predicting a flood is more difficult than it sounds.

In the first place, the cloud that produces a cloudburst (see page 49) is always one among many clouds. Any one of them might cause torrential rain, but only some of them will, and the culprits are not easy to identify. Nor does a cloudburst necessarily mean there will be floods. It depends where the rain falls. If it falls on level ground it may cause no problems, but if it falls over hills and the water drains into narrow valleys, these may flood. If the "cloudburst cloud" is difficult to identify, it is even more difficult to figure out precisely where it will be when it releases its water.

Obviously, flood prediction must begin with weather forecasting. Meteorologists at the National Meteorological Center track weather systems all over the world, using satellite images and measurements as well as regular reports from surface weather stations, ships, and aircraft. When meteorologists believe a particular system might produce rain heavy or prolonged enough to cause flooding, they notify the river forecasting center concerned. In the United States there are 13 of these centers, each covering a very large area and several drainage basins. There, scientists calculate the risk of floods should their area receive the amount of rain forecast. This information is then sent to state and local weather forecasting offices to be used in conjunction with the information from the National Meteorological Center. If necessary, watches and warnings are issued. Most countries operate a similar system for flood prediction and warning.

Hydrologists, the scientists who study the way water moves through and over the ground, relate the weather forecast to what they know about the area in which the rain is expected to fall. Part of their investigation is historical. Many people measure the rainfall near their homes, and some send their records to their national meteorological service. Measuring rainfall is not difficult: Experiment 30 in volume 6 tells you how to make a simple rain gauge and do this for yourself.

Records of rainfall have been kept for many years, and so have records of floods. By comparing past floods with the amount and duration of rainfall that preceded them, it is possible to make a rough estimate of the kind of weather likely to cause flooding.

Records of river levels, although they do not go back very far, are now being compiled and are very important. They are made at "gauging stations" along rivers. A pipe below ground connects a chamber in the station to a borehole beside the river. Water flows into the chamber and reaches the same height as the water in the river, but it is not disturbed by waves or currents, so the height can be read easily and accurately. The principle underlying the technique is identical to that of the Nilometer, which has been used for centuries to monitor the water level in the Nile (see page 32). The

Figure 34: *An employee of the Water Resources Division of the U.S. Geological Survey measures the rate of flow of a stream with a current meter suspended on a wading rod.*
(U.S. Geological Survey/ J. R. Stacy)

Figure 35: *Gauging Station on Battle Creek, near Cottonwood, California, is isolated by floodwaters, December 22, 1964.* (U.S. Geological Survey/ A. O. Waananen)

same device also provides information about the height of the water table. These levels are monitored constantly by an automatic device. In older installations they are recorded, often at 15-minute intervals, by holes punched in a roll of paper; the roll is collected for examination. More modern stations transmit data directly to a central point. These data reveal almost immediately the slightest change in the river level or water table.

Combined with information about rainfall, records gathered over a number of years can also be used in another way. They make it possible to calculate how long it takes for rain in a drainage basin to reach the river under different conditions of soil moisture. Two flows are involved. One is the "storm flow," of water running directly over the surface. Obviously, it will reach the river first. The other is the "base flow," of water that percolates downward through the soil and travels downhill as part of the groundwater. The storm and base flows give a value for the "time-to-peak," which is the time that elapses between the onset of heavy rain and the maximum water level in rivers. Once these figures are known for drainage basins that are well monitored, the calculations can be applied to other drainage basins, where the rocks and soils are similar but there are few or no instruments to make actual measurements.

Even then, the data are usually insufficient to allow the prediction of rare floods—the kind that can be expected only once in 50,000 years, or longer—because accurate records have not been kept for long enough. To make predictions of this kind, the available data must be used in the construction of models.

Some water-flow models are physical. Miniature hills and rivers are built and water poured into them to see what conditions cause floods. Flood defenses are also tested with models before they are built. Small-scale models of dams, spillways (see page 112), and river embankments are subjected to different volumes of water traveling at different speeds, with instruments measuring the currents and turbulence in the water and the force it exerts on various parts of the structures. In real rivers, colored dyes (harmless to wildlife) are used to track the speed and direction of water flow.

Computer models are also used. These display their results as pictures, supported by long printouts of numbers. Despite the pictures, these models are entirely mathematical, and the mathematics are highly complex. Numbers are fed into the model for the height of the water table, the amount of moisture held in the soil above the water table, the characteristics of the soil and underlying rock, the rate of groundwater flow, the amount of rain, the capacity of rivers, and many more factors. These are then related to one another by sets of equations.

Physical models are limited to actual present-day conditions and structures, but a computer model allows scientists more freedom. If they feed in actual data from weather that did and did not produce flooding in the past and the model predicts accurately the floods that really occurred, the conditions can be altered. Rainfall can be prolonged and made more intense to see what conditions would be necessary to trigger a very rare flood. It is only a calculation, of course, and no such flood has actually happened, but should those conditions occur in the real world the model calculations will give ample warning of the scale of flooding that might happen.

Once a reliable model has been compiled of the movement of water through a drainage basin, the model is kept up to date. The model allows for the rate at which rivers carry water out of the basin, so feeding in the amount and distribution of rainfall as it happens means the model always represents the actual amount, location, and rate of movement of water, and what the model tells the scientists can be checked against the situation in the real world outside, so corrections can be made when necessary.

Everyone who might be affected needs to be warned, but some people may require more information. Farmers, for example, need to know not only whether their fields are likely to be flooded, but for how long they will remain under water. Emergency services need to know the probable depth of the floodwater. Will they need boats to rescue people and, if so, what kind of boats? If temporary accommodation is required for those evacuated from their homes, for how long will these remain in use? Such information can also be calculated from the state of the area as recorded by the model.

Along coasts, the risk of flooding comes from the sea as well as from rivers. Storm and tidal surges (see page 64) can be predicted more simply than river overflows, because they do not involve the movement of water below ground. Storms are observed closely as they move across the ocean and, with the help of satellite images and measurements from specially equipped airplanes, forecasters are now able to measure their intensity long before the storms cross a coast. Scientists can tell the size of waves a storm will generate, and relating their arrival to the state of the tide is not difficult.

Tsunamis (see page 54) can also be predicted. Most are caused by earthquakes below the ocean floor, although less severe tsunamis are also caused by seabed volcanic eruptions and the slumping of sediments down slopes. Earthquakes produce shock waves, called "seismic" waves, that are detected within minutes by seismic stations all over the world. Information about them is then passed to the Pacific Tsunami Warning Center in Hawaii and the Alaska Tsunami Warning Center in Palmer, Alaska, where it is processed to predict where a tsunami may strike and its severity.

Flood prediction is not perfect, but it is sufficiently reliable for its warnings to be heeded. All flooding of farmland and urban areas causes damage, but at one time it also caused many deaths. Prediction has greatly increased the chance of human survival.

Safety

If you live on low ground near a river or coast, your home could be at risk from flooding. Find out the height of your home above sea or river level.

The history of your neighborhood will provide a useful guide to the extent of the risk. If your family has lived in the same place for many years, you will know whether there have been floods during that time. If you arrived recently, the local library and newspaper will have records of any past floods, and staff at the nearest office of the National Weather Service will know whether floods are likely. They, and staff at the local branch of the American Red Cross, emergency management, and civil defense offices will tell you what kind of weather emergencies occur in your area and what plans have been made for responding to them. During any emergency, events happen quickly. You will have little time to act, and you must know what to do.

You may have to leave your home. Arrange with everyone living with you a safe place to meet outside on high ground in case you are dispersed. Arrange with a friend or relative who lives far enough away not to be affected by your emergency to act as a contact. If you are dispersed, telephone the contact, who will then know where everyone is. Make sure young children know how to use the telephone and can dial 911. If you are warned of an emergency, write down the contact number and make sure everyone carries a copy. Teach everyone how to turn off the water, electricity, and gas supply.

Keep a can opener and a store of enough canned food to last everyone for three days. Floodwater will contaminate any exposed food it touches. Your emergency supplies should also include a portable radio and flashlight, with spare batteries for both, a set of car keys, cash or a credit card, a first aid kit, and any items needed for infants or people with special requirements. Store these supplies in strong bags you can grab quickly and carry easily. Nearby, keep rubber boots for everyone. When you receive a Watch alert, add to these supplies a sleeping bag or blanket and one complete change of clothes for each person.

When the warning comes, you are most likely to hear it first on the radio or television. The National Weather Service broadcasts local forecasts and warnings continuously, which can be received by NOAA Weather Radios, usually over a range of about 40 miles. You can buy a weather radio that runs on both electric power and batteries and has an alert tone which sounds automatically if a Watch or Warning is being broadcast. Whether you use a weather radio or ordinary radio or television, once a Watch or Warning has been issued, leave the receiver on, so you will be kept up to date.

The first message will be a Flood Watch or Flash Flood Watch. This means a flood or flash flood is possible in your area within the next few hours. When you hear a Watch announcement, check your emergency stores. If the power fails, gas station pumps may be out of action, so make sure your automobile has a full tank. Fill the bathtub and clean containers with water. You will need 3 gallons for each person. In the case of a Flash Flood Watch, be ready to leave home at a moment's notice. If you plan to drive to safety, load your supplies in the car.

Next, you may hear an Urban and Small Stream Advisory. This means small streams and rivers are overflowing. Low-lying areas, including road and railroad underpasses and some streets, are under water, and water is flowing back from some storm drains. The problem is not serious, but you should avoid the places affected. If there are children in your household, make sure you know where they are. Do not let them play outdoors where they could be caught in the floodwater.

Alternatively, you may hear a Flood Warning. This means serious flooding has started or is imminent nearby. If you are on low ground, move to high ground. If you delay, your escape route may be cut off by floods. If the broadcasts advise you to evacuate your home, grab your emergency supplies and leave at once.

If you hear a Flash Flood Warning, the danger is serious. It may not be raining where you are, but do not let this deceive you. There has been very heavy rain, probably a cloudburst, in nearby hills, and the water is flowing across the surface in your direction. A flash flood can advance as a wall of muddy, turbulent water, trees, rocks, and other debris, up to 20 feet high and traveling at the speed of a train. If you are on low ground, leave at once for high ground. Do not delay. You may have only seconds to escape.

Storm surges also cross coasts suddenly and can carry water some distance inland, cutting off escape routes. Warnings of severe storms or hurricanes will also warn of the expected storm surge. Follow the instructions you are given and if you are advised to evacuate your home, do so immediately.

Tsunamis are rare events, but if one approaches people in coastal areas will receive a Tsunami Warning. Treat this like a Flash Flood Warning and leave at once, heading inland. Do not attempt to return home until you hear over the radio or from officials that it is safe to do so.

Once you are outdoors, remember that the key to survival is to keep away from the floodwaters. Go to the highest spot you can find.

Do not try to cross floodwater on foot or in a car. If the water reaches your ankles, turn back and find another route. The road may have been washed away beneath the water, which may be much deeper than it looks. If the car stalls in water, do not try to restart it. Leave it at once and head for high ground. The water does not need to rise very far before the car will float away, out of control. If you try to escape then you may find it difficult, or impossible, to fight against the currents. Be especially careful at night. Visibility may be poor in heavy rain, making flooded dips and hollows difficult to see.

Never pitch a tent or park a trailer or camper close to a river or along a stream, arroyo, or wash, especially if there are dark clouds in the sky. A cloudburst can turn a dry stream bed into a raging torrent in a matter of seconds. When choosing a camping place, also remember that heavy rain can trigger mudslides and landslides. Avoid camping near the foot of a steep slope.

If you hear of floods, but are not affected by them directly, keep away from the flooded area. You may have friends or relatives whom you would like to assist, but emergency services will be on the scene already. They are trained and equipped to provide the help needed, and you will either be in their way or get into difficulties yourself and need their help. If food, blankets, or other help is needed, an appeal will be broadcast and you will be told the location of collection points.

When the floodwaters recede, you will be able to move downstairs if you have been trapped indoors. If you have had to evacuate, you will be told when it is safe to return home.

Floodwater is filthy. It carries mud and debris everywhere, and you should assume it is contaminated with raw sewage. If it has entered your home it will have made a great deal of mess, but you will be able to see clearly the height it reached.

Destroy all food that has come into contact with the water. It will not be safe to eat. A refrigerator door should be watertight, and if you have been away for only a day or two at least some of the food inside it may be fit to eat. When you open the door it will be immediately obvious if water has penetrated. If it has, discard all the food.

Do not drink tap water or use it for cooking without boiling it first. If your water comes from a well, it must be pumped out and, as the well refills, tested for bacterial or other contamination. You must not drink it or use it for cooking until you know it is safe. If you are not sure how to check its safety, your local public health authority will advise you.

Do not turn on the electricity supply or try to use any electrical appliance until all the wiring has dried thoroughly and been checked for safety. Check gas pipes for breaks before reconnecting the supply. When entering any building, do not use naked flames to help you see. There could be flammable gases trapped inside, and a single spark could cause an explosion. Make a note of any power or telephone lines that are down and report them to the appropriate authority.

If you need medical assistance, go to the nearest hospital. If you need first aid, food, clothing, or shelter, contact the Red Cross.

Provided you listen to and act on them, official Watch and Warning announcements can save your life, but you should be alert to the risk of floods at all times. Cloudbursts are associated with thunderstorms. If you hear thunder over the distant hills, turn on the radio. A flood could be on its way. If you live near a river, watch its level after heavy rain and start preparing for a flood if you see it rising. Warnings will be broadcast if a tsunami is heading for your stretch of coast, but watch the sea. If a wave rises up the shore more than about 3 feet (0.9 meter) higher than the one before it, the water level remains high for a couple of minutes before the water flows back, and then the sea retreats much farther than usual, it is likely that a tsunami will arrive very soon. Move at once to high ground well away from the shore.

Of all the catastrophes severe weather can cause, floods are by far the most devastating and dangerous. They can and do lead to loss of life. Yet with adequate preparation and warning, people who carry out a sensible plan without panic have a very good chance of surviving unharmed. It may be impossible to prevent a flood from destroying or damaging your property, but there is no need to let it take your life.

Index

Italic numbers indicate illustrations.